Country

by A Farmer's Wife

Illustrated by Mandi Madden

I am very grateful to the Courier for giving me permission to reproduce these articles, which first appeared in print on the Farming page of that newspaper, and for allowing me to use the photograph on the front cover.

I would also like to thank The Editor, Mr. Adrian Arthur, The Farming Editor, Mr. Andrew Arbuckle, and The Features Editor, Mrs. Shona Lorimer, for the encouragement I have received during my two and a half years of writing Country Matters, and for all the help and support I've been given during the publishing of this book.

To Jean — with best wishes from Shelu Garduie .. "The Farmer's wife" ..

Printed and published by A. & A. Slinger, Forfar.

Forebears

Foreword

I have often heard it said that everyone has a book inside their head, but, if it hadn't been for my family and the friendly folks at A. & A. Slinger the printers, that's where mine would still be.

My dear Aberdeenshire Daughter-in-law, who's no stranger to the world of publishing, suggested that I should make my articles into a book, and so, here it is. A book, you could say, that was written by a woman out standing in her field.

Now, first of all I'm very grateful to everyone at A. & A. Slinger's for suffering my dottings out and in, but, my special thanks must go to the Manager, Alastair Donald, who has put the whole show on the road, and to Mandi Madden for her wonderful art work. The tears of laughter ran down my cheeks the first time I saw her interpretations of my stories.

And of course, I have to thank my family ..... the family who have unwittingly provided me with enough material to last a lifetime, and who are as follows:

Bruin One and her husband - the Nurse and the Salmon Fisher.

Bruin Two, his wife and their little daughter - The Troot Fisher, The Quinie and Wee Baby Bear.

Bruin Three - The Singin' Bothy Loon,

And last, but not least, in a league of his own Bruin Four - The Fitba' Loon.

In the generations beyond there's Grandfather Bear and his dear friend and companion Auntie Bear.

And finally, there's the man who read the proofs. The man, who through no fault of his own, has become a legend in his own lifetime. The man whose suffering is only surpassed by that of his wife. The man whose trials and tribulations are broadcast to the whole world. Yes, the one and only Father Bear.

And, at the tail end, there's Buffy the 'auld wifie's' cat.

* * *

The Story Teller

Once upon a time there was a little girl who lived with her mother and father and auntie in an old farm house in the glen, where the clouds of summer midgies danced high above the big brown burn and the aurora borealis flitted across the frosty winter skies.

The child spent her early years listening to the stories and songs and music of all the good folk who came in to her warm, lamp lit kitchen and thought — maybe, just maybe, when I'm a grown up lady I'll be able to do some of these things too.

Well, after many many moons had come and gone, and a lot of water had passed under the Troll's bridge, she fell in with a band of storytellers who said, "Come with us and we will make you rich."

"Oh no," she replied sadly, "I cannot do that because I am a farmer's wife, and my husband and my children would not manage without me, but, I promise I will write more stories, and once a year I will come and tell them to you."

She kept her promise, but as time passed by, and when she was growing quite old, she began to think again.

Maybe, just maybe, if I ask very nicely, I might be allowed to write for a newspaper — the one that used to have Billy and Bunny in it when I was little.

Well, she did ask very nicely, and the newspaper lady thought for a little while and then she said: "Yes, you can write your stories on our Farming Page," and that, as they say in all good stories, is how it all began.

Memories From The Berry Field

It's berry time again, and this year, at long last, we have our own strawberries which have the most gloriously sweet, squelchy, dripping down the chin taste I've ever come across. We have a net over them, but this hasn't hindered the resident fat blackbird who sits tutting at us, from having a field day. I don't really grudge him a few berries, but he's done more sampling than Goldilocks. Of course, he's not alone. There are many sets of large treaded footprints leading to that secluded spot in the garden, and Father Bear has suggested that I should tally up all the pounds of berries we pick, and see what the yield has been from our four metre square crop. Why do I feel that somewhere in the not too distant future I could be spending my July days sitting in a little wooden hut with a set of scales and a big P.Y.O. sign waiting for the world and his wife to arrive with an assortment of empty ice-cream boxes and bad backs?

When I was young, in the days when the dinosaurs roamed the earth, there was only one field of rasps in our part of the country and the crowds would flock along the road like a scene from an epic film. Some on foot, pushing prams, while older, weary children cried out for a hurl, the majority on bikes, and a few who chugged by in Ford Eights and Prefects with their heads in the air.

Everyone was there for the money except one proud, highland lady from a little cottage up the glen, who let it be known she was there for the fresh air and who changed into a clean peeny before leaving the field. A family whose numbers were on a par with The Broons arrived with great commotion and blue reek in an ancient shooting brake tied together with wire and rope and sporting the most vivid green tarpaulin roof you've ever seen. They were kindly folk and the mother, who was of more than ample proportions, was an easy going, canny body who harmed no-one.

Now, as an only child who'd led a somewhat restricted life on an upland farm, I'd had to listen to all mothers do's and don'ts before I was allowed to go to the berries on my own. She wanted no reports of any misdemeanours, like the time her daughter, along with the rest of the school (twelve in all) had been caught flicking custard ceilingwards with their spoons in a little impromptu competition! I dutifully answered yes and no in all the right places and then I was allowed to shoot off on my bike with my schoolbag full of jam pieces and a flask.

As I sped downhill towards the village through clouds of dancing midgies and damp spiders' webs I felt happy and free and boy, was I going to be the talk of the place as I raced up and down the dreels like a streak of greased lightning.

However, my bravado began to evaporate as I shyly joined all the other experienced pickers, because I'd really no idea how to get started and they obviously did. A kindly woman took me under her wing as I stood at the side of the field, and in no time at all I felt like an old hand.

Here, this is easy, I thought. This was independence, I could be rich, I might even earn a whole pound, but a quick calculation showed that I'd need to pick one hundred and twenty pounds of rasps to do that.

Some of the village children began to monkey about and throw berries in my direction, but I ignored them. Dedication was the name of this game.

My ears worked overtime listening to the many and diverse conversations which were on the go, and if one of them was becoming exciting, I nipped up or down the dreel to listen to the end of it. From time to time the lady on the other side of the bushes would chat to me, but I was really perfectly happy in this little world of cheery banter and sunshine. I only took ten minutes to wolf down my boring, blackcurrant jam pieces and drink my tea. It's funny how tea always tastes so good in the open air. The young folk, who'd decided I was a total waste of time, had gone to chase each other round a field of hay coles. When I lugged my heavy pails up to the final weigh-in I tripped over somebody's berries and sent them scattering all over the place. This salvage job took at least ten minutes and I slunk discreetly away from the scene of the crime.

The magic moment arrived, I'd made a pound and three pence. Yippee! I just couldn't wait to get home with my wonderful news. I heched and peched up all the steep hills on my bike which seemed to have grown wings, and as I rushed into the kitchen, did I not drop my flask on the stone floor. I picked up the tinkling object and waited for mother's reaction. Surprisingly, she said very little, but the noise woke up father who'd been snorting and snoring behind his paper. After he'd digested my news and praised my efforts he asked me to get my tea as quickly as I could because he needed a hand to brand seventy sheep.

SHEEP! SHEEP! BLOOMIN SHEEP! I'd been an unpaid dog's deputy most of my life, and tonight, I, Queen of the raspfield, or at least the Princess, was expected to go and stand wielding a hissing, hot iron among clouds of acrid smoke, branding seventy stupid sheep. What a come down. Ah, but wait a minute, maybe a bit of negotiating could be done here, say, tuppence a horn, or even at the lower rate of a penny a horn. Was it worth a try? Was it fiddlesticks. I might have known he'd mention the flask.

Yellow Peril Strikes Again

A blast of music from the radio alarm drags me into a dull, damp, misty morning, and as I lie there trying to focus my mind on the events of the day ahead and watch a spider tearing frantically across the ceiling to some poor, trapped victim, I suddenly remember with a sinking heart why I set the alarm for 4.00 a.m. - the rape and pillage is about to begin, and Father Bear is still dead to the world.

Are you picturing great hunks of bearded Viking manhood with their longboat over their muscular shoulders, tramping up the farm road on their thick, leather thonged legs, singing four part harmony songs with a few reluctant ostriches in tow? Well, forget the romantic nonsense and let's get down to the serious subject of oilseed rape, the crop which brings tears to many people's eyes, and sends them racing for their hankies and their nasal sprays as they pass its sunshiny yellow fields dotted, patchwork quilt like, over the late spring countryside.

Now, I don't personally suffer from the rape when it's blooming, it's the blooming cutting of the stuff I suffer from, and I'll tell you why.

Many years ago this strange looking, blue and white metal amphibian like creature with staring eyes and outstretched arms came racing erratically into our close, having been bought at a roup by Father Bear, who was clinging on to the helm like grim death, and suffering from first degree sea-sickness. As he threw open the door of the cramped, glass cab and clambered unsteadily down to the ground, he proudly announced that this was a rape-swather.

Before long, this weird newcomer was joined by two equally weird looking workmates, all displaying their own individual personalities. The two blue and white ones always appeared to be smiling and happy, whereas the sickly, pea-green coloured one (like the owl and the pussycat's boat) appeared dour and sullen, but then, maybe it had become disenchanted with folk always turning its name into a swearword as they struggled to pronounce it.

Well, mid-July duly arrived, bringing with it orders for swathing, and co-drivers who, luckily for us, had a working knowledge of machinery and a good sense of humour. One chap insisted that his swather either loved or loathed bikes, because it made a beeline for every one it passed on the road.

Lucky me, who was on holiday, was enlisted to help with the fetching, the flashing, and the manning of the phone, in these fraught days before we possessed mobile phones and an answering machine. Father Bear well and truly warned me to make sure I got all the details correct, like the acreage, the directions, and the exact field location from any potential customers who rang. It wasn't slow to dawn on me that I could make a complete pig's ear out of the whole enterprise if I wasn't very careful and I had this worrying picture in my mind of our taskforce in not only the wrong field, but on the wrong farm, being pursued, Charlie Chaplin like, by a very angry farmer and his collies.

Every second phone call seemed to be an S.O.S. from the troops to sort our swather or send over someone - pronto. (Nowadays, we have the good fortune to be able to phone direct from the field to the consultant surgeon of swathers and all things mechanical. This unfailingly cheerful lad races around the country in his familiar van, bringing sanity to the stressed, and even fish suppers to the starving stranded.)

Now, I became sort of scunnered with the fetching lark, which nine times out ot ten landed me in some unwarranted kind of trouble as you will see. One night in the ever-deepening twilight among the high hedges of the fertile carse lands, Grandpa Bear, the two younger Bruins and yours truly spent three hours in maze-like conditions trying to locate a swather. When we bumped slowly over the main line railway level-crossing for the fifth time, we began to feel like something out of a Carry on film (dare I say "Carry On Swathing") and when we eventually found it, we were told - "You've taken that long we've decided to call it a day."

The most memorable "fetch" of all (and there were many) was the time when Father Bear had instructed me to pick him up beside the biggest hangar on an old airfield at 11.30 p.m. Eventually, I found the place and parked the car beside what, in my opinion, was the biggest hangar. As darkness fell quickly around me and blotted out the landscape, I began to panic. Where was he? It was well after midnight and there was still no sign of him. I started the car and drove about twenty yards up the grassy road. My headlights picked up a man pacing back and forwards. It was him, and boy, was he in a rage. In fact, I'm certain if he'd just waved his arms up and down, he could have taken off on the old runway.

I quite enjoyed the escorting trips when I went on ahead of the swather with fullbeam headlamps and hazard lights flashing, warning oncoming drivers to ca'canny. Most folk were quite reasonable about this and pulled into the side, but there were always the Hooray Hendrys, who went swishing past in a cloud of stoor and rattled gravel on the side of my car. However, I got great satisfaction watching their comeuppance in my mirror as they met the impatient, high powered, whining swather face to face in a brilliant glow of tail-lights and a squealing of brakes. I became quite competent at lip reading on my travels, but the question on every driver's lips was usually "what the devil is that" or words to that effect!

When I arrived home again after these little social outings, I still had to find time to shop, wash, clean and cook. I made enough pieces to feed the proverbial five thousand, filled countless bottles of juice, prepared an evening meal and strode goose-step like, through rape stubble which resembled a field of sharp pencils, to replenish supplies. As the saying goes "When the going gets tough, the tough get going."

Do you know where I would have loved to have gone, and where the going was really tough? With the Pioneers who blazed the trails across America to Oregon and California. I would have been up there on my conestoga wagon, a big, fearless, flint eyed woman, with steel in her bones and fire in her soul, driving on through the Humbolt Sink, scattering the Sioux and staking her territory. Yep, The Woman Who Won The West.

Ach well, I suppose I'd better waken Big Chief Swathing Bear and escort him out east in the little red wagon. I just hope it starts.

* * *

Memories of a Life Time Spent in Piece Making

Were you one of the folk with a lump in your throat last week as you watched your little hand-reared pet being driven off to pastures new? Did you picture the wee figure standing in a strange enclosure, with an ever vigilant collie circling around? Was there a tear in your eye when the sturdy little legs came bouncing out of the pen at 12.30 p.m. excitedly waving a picture that would have made Van Gogh reach for his cool shades, and declaring that school was ace, Granny's juice was yuk and Wayne had wet his trousers?

I may as well be honest here and admit I'm delighted these days are behind me, and that, thankfully, my four Bruins are beyond the age of returning to school after "The far ower long summer holidays thae teachers get." In fact, I've often wondered if I might have been eligible for a mention in that world famous book of records, because, when my youngest Bruin left the school over two years ago, Father Time's Scythe had swathed through 26 years of my life.

Now, these 26 years began with the "flower power" and "peace man" days of the "swinging sixties" and ended in the Internet nineties with hi-tech trainers and posh piece boxes.

It will probably come as no surprise to you, therefore, to hear that I'm heartily sick of making up pieces. I reckon I've made up enough pieces (with every kind of filling known to man) to cover half the county and beyond. The Bruins' school pieces, Father and Grandfather Bears' pieces, harvest pieces, dainty pieces for fund raising do's, and so on. When I pass on to that big green field in the sky, I'm going to leave behind me a loaf shaped headstone, with an epitaph along the lines of "Here lies a woman who spent a lifetime giving bread to the hungry. May she rest in peace."

Furthermore, I've said to our minister that when I reach the pearly gates, St. Peter will be standing there waiting for me with a loaf in one hand and a pound of boiled ham in the other. When I was little, in the days before sliced bread, my mother sometimes put cold meat on my school pieces (before school dinners reached the wild frontier). Now I didn't like cold meat, so I hunted around the grassy playground of our little country school for sourocks, (little edible green leaves with a tartish taste) and, when I found them, I flung the meat over the dyke or gave it to the little janitresse's big dog. Then I filled my bread with the juicy greenery and munched it up quite happily.

The back to school clothing was something else though. All the adverts show smart, smiling faced little children wearing neat uniforms, but they never show you the torn faced teenagers you've dragged off a tractor to go shopping, do they? Why do farm menfolk (old and young) have such a spite at shopping? They'll trail quite happily round a roup in the pouring rain and wait for hours to bid for what they've had their eye on. But clothes shopping - oh, no. Over the years I've brought home enough clothes to kit out a regiment, and all I get are a few grunts, which usually means they fit. My mother once stood behind an elderly country couple who were looking at trousers in a shop window. "Hoo wid thae dae ye Wullie?" asked the wife pointing to a particular pair. "Och jist please yersel Jean," was the reply.

Apart from all the school clothes buying, there was, needless to say, the washing of it, and I suppose if I'd been good at maths (and I'm not), I might have got quite a kick out of calculating how many skirts, shirts and pairs of school trousers I'd washed over the 26 years, and how many tons of soap powder I'd used. Maybe I should have contacted the family at No. 10 (no, not them) because, I've always been impressed by the practical methods they used to solve Horace's homework problems.

As well as the new clothing and shoes, the Bruins usually got their "August stocking fillers" like fancy rubbers, pencil cases that looked like packets of crisps, multicoloured pens and folders with trendy covers which were all designed to entice them to return to the classroom.

Not that it worked, because they had far too much to do at home at this time of year. After all, hadn't they waited nearly eleven months for a shot of the combine and a chance to drive bogey loads of grain back to the steading? They could even argue that this was maths at ground level. When we lived further away from school than we did latterly, they grilled me all the way home in the car about what had been happening during their absence. However, when we moved to a farm within a mile of the school, they must have spent a fair part of the day looking out of the classroom windows, for they were able to tell me what had been happening.

I can remember not being too fussed about going to school, because, I never wearied at home, and when my new teacher (a real mother hen) came to pay me a pre-school visit (I think she'd been taken out for a run by a nephew or someone and decided to call on us) I was really far too busy playing at houses with our three cats to have much time to spend with her. A lad who helped us with the sheep, and whose serious expression belied leg pulling, said he often went along to play leap-frog with her in the evenings and I had a mental picture of this stout, three years off retiring, maiden lady with four chins and a grey bun, tearing breathlessly down the hill and soaring over his bent shoulders with her long skirt and cardigan flapping around her.

Oh dear, that's the blooming phone again. It's Father Bear roaring down the mobile from somewhere around the Niagara Falls. They're needing more drinks and pieces, and could I nip along the road and inform the other combine driver which field he's to head for next? Oh, and by the way, could I go and get a fish supper for him while I'm in for 20 kingsize?

Did I mention that this year it was my turn to leave the chalk face? If one more well-meaning soul kindly enquires how I'm enjoying early retirement I might just tell them.

* * *

Experience Not To Be Sniffed At

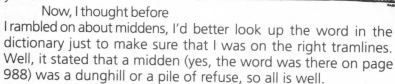

I've often said that if I wrote a book I'd call it the "Singing Dunghill" or "Music Over The Midden," and when I tell people this they always laugh, but they probably think I'm a piece short of a mid yokin'.

Now, I thought before I rambled on about middens, I'd better look up the word in the dictionary just to make sure that I was on the right tramlines. Well, it stated that a midden (yes, the word was there on page 988) was a dunghill or a pile of refuse, so all is well.

When I was little, in the days before there were forty flavours of crisps, our cattle dung midden sprawled out in all its glory behind the byre, and, one wonderful day when we had some toonsers visiting us, their little girl slid down from her chair after she'd finished her tea, and returned ten minutes later cradling a decaying hen which she laid gently down on the hand embroidered tablecloth among the best china. I nearly choked trying not to laugh as mother squawked at father to "Get that filthy beast off the table and bury it in the midden, which you should have done in the first place." The child was quite unperturbed, but father wasn't when he went out with the hen and found the three year old's fingers had also managed to turn on the tap of a full tank of paraffin, and most of it had run down the close.

Sometimes when father went to visit his neighbours for a chinwag, he took me with him, and one day, as they stood blethering away about all the usual boring things, I was warned not to go too near the edge of the farm's impressively-high dung midden. Well, I still don't know what happened, but a few seconds later I found myself hurtling (like Damien and his hens' feathers wings) through the air to the most undignified landing of my life. The farmers' two elderly sisters tried to clean me up, but as I stood reeking and dripping in their stone floored kitchen, I knew I was beyond human aid. My hairy green pleated tweed skirt, which should have had a government health warning, looked like a graipful of silage, and on the way home, as I sat on a thick newspaper in the back of the car with all the windows open, father told me to play down the disaster as much as possible - he knew he'd get the blame. He was right.

My next close encounter of the midden kind came to pass many years later with the incident of the hens' slurry, when poor Father Bear had experienced "one of those days". To cut a long story slightly shorter, he ended up shovelling the slittery stuff out the back door of our biggest shed of laying hens, into a bogie. Now, I was going to the two older Bruins' parents' evening, and after I'd dressed myself in the smart but casual clothes, with a scarf flung carelessly over my shoulder, I gingerly picked my way round to where he was working to say "cheerio". There were a couple of steps going down into the shed, and as I couldn't see him in the dim light, I waited at the side of the evil smelling bogie until I heard him approaching, and then I shouted "I'm ...." but, before I could say "away" a great shoveful of the cocktail came flying up out of the shed, and with a great splash, landed into the frothy brew. I was rooted to the spot, and dripping from head to toe when poor Father Bear's sweaty face appeared. "Honestly, I never knew you were there," he gasped.

In due course, we said an unemotional farewell to our hardworking little red hens, hitched up our wagons, and headed further north to a land where the warm, west wind whispered gently over the braes and brought with it the sweet scents of summer meadows, or at least it did until Father Bear inherited an endless supply of broiler dung with its top of the range, five star smell.

Now, I tell you this, there is no hope of anonymity if you possess a broiler dung midden at the side of a dual carriageway because every Tom, Dick and Auntie Harriet will comment on the "fowl" smell. In fact, it became, and still is, a strong topic of local conversation. "What on earth is that you folk are spreading on the fields?" or "Here, I dinnae ken whit that is on your fields, but it fairly maks yer een water," or, "Ma grandchildren were gey near seek last Setterday when we passed your fields wie oor car windies open." (You will understand that I am toning down the strength of the language somewhat). There was no respite either from the smell of the stuff because when I went into the nearby town, little groups of weekend shoppers were discussing the possible source of "That awfy stink," as I slunk past with my dark specs and balaclava and "It's us" printed on my forehead.

So, you will now begin to understand why I've earned my First Class Honours Degree in Middenology, and how I can name that pong in one. There are, of course, those who have challenged me that pigs' dung has the worst smell of all, but I pooh pooh this. In fact I'd only rank it as a three star smell.

And, to get back to my book title. Well, I've always had the good fortune to be surrounded by music, and can't you just picture the wonderfully, eye-catching cover with it's authentic scratch and sniff panel which can only add to the enjoyment of the contents?.

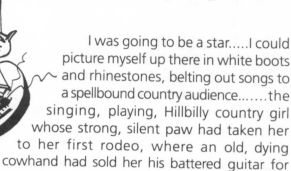

Sheep Sales

I was going to be a star.....I could picture myself up there in white boots and rhinestones, belting out songs to a spellbound country audience.......the singing, playing, Hillbilly country girl whose strong, silent paw had taken her to her first rodeo, where an old, dying cowhand had sold her his battered guitar for five dollars. Now, I'm maybe stretching things a bit, but a girl can dream, can't she?

The hard facts were that I went to the September sheep sales with father, who was a real soft touch, (especially after he'd had a dram) and persuaded him to give me my 'shepherding' money so that I could buy a guitar.

"Well," he enquired, when I caught up with him and his drouthy cronies among the sheep pens "Are ye happy noo you've got your banjo?" The comments as I proudly humphed it around were just what you'd have expected. "O, look, here's a lassie wie a banjo," (it was always a banjo) "How aboot playin' us a tune." Play, that was a joke. I was so naive I didn't even realise the bloomin' thing came untuned, and the D.I.Y. tutor book I'd invested in resembled a plan of a hydro-electric power station! However, I promised myself that I'd sit in the back of the car on the way home and suss it all out. (The confidence of youth is a wonderful thing, isn't it?)

That plan went out the window with the news that two of our neighbouring farmers, who'd come in with someone else in the morning, were needing a lift home. When I saw the pair of them "Fou, an' unco happy" lurching towards us with their raincoats over their shoulders, and their crooks clattering across the cobbles, I realised there would be no shortage of music. Of course, their gratitude was quite overwhelming, and they nearly broke my fingers with their enthusiastic handshakes. With the maximum of difficulty they got into the car and duly admired the 'banjo' which put them in the mood for a song.Without further ado they launched into "Bonnie Dundee" and with the reckless abandon of the inebriated, began flinging their bunnets all over the place.

As we rattled along the middle of the road (father always drove in the middle) he said he thought we were running out of oil, (well, the car was anyway) so, we drew into a filling station where one of the passengers insisted again and again that it was better to run out of petrol than oil, whilst his sidekick tried to play the 'banjo'. It was just as well they were happy on the journey because we all knew the Tam O'Shanter welcome that awaited them. I really enjoyed those hilarious trips and I knew if I clyped I might not get back again, so mother never knew the half of it.

Looking back, I think I must have been about five or six when I started going to the sheep sales, and over the years I spent many happy hours wandering out and in the different rings, climbing up the tiered rows of wooden seats to get a better view of what was going on (especially if our sheep were in the ring), and sitting down among all the grownups to a really good three course dinner nicely set out on a thick, white tablecloth anchored down with heavy cutlery and jugs of water. Mother's silly idea of a mid day meal out was fish and chips and bread and butter accompanied by a pot of stewed tea, and NO PUDDING! This she ordered in her poshest voice, totally ignoring my pleas for decent food.

The local contractor normally transported our sheep to and from the market, and I always felt sad when I saw their black noses and glittering eyes looking fearfully out at us from between the wooden spars of the float as it dragged its heavy load up the brae and disappeared round the corner. The owner's son, who usually collected our sheep, had been courting my cousin, but, sadly, it was unrequited love, and she said to her parents that she was going to tell him so. "Haud on, Haud on," protested her father, "at least wait 'til I get ma yowes awa."

And to get back on this auld yowe, did I ever find my fame and fortune? Well, no, not yet, but someday me an' my banjo'll be beltin' out "Your Bleatin Heart" from that great sale-ring in the sky.

* * *

Back Through The Mists Of Memory

Last week was one of those weeks. The youngest Bruin was in hospital recovering from a back operation. Father Bear was driving tatties at the other end of the world and his temperamental, but hard working little red wagon went into one of its huffs because he was thoughtless enough to be contemplating its replacement when it was bringing him home. It's always had this nasty little streak, and after emitting a few puffs of smoke from under its bonnet, and destroying some of its electric wiring it had to be hauled unceremoniously home by tractor. Now, the result of this little hiccup landed on my doorstep as I suspected it would, and the following morning, I was back in the house before 8 a.m. after a 40 mile round delivery trip.

The members of the dawn chorus were still clearing their little throats when Father Bear and I sped along through the spooky September mists and watched the sun's sullen face glow red from exertion whilst he struggled to throw off his thick, fleecy blankets of grey. I almost felt we were on a Safari trip when shadowy deer tripped daintily across the road in front of us and clusters of pheasants stood shaking their heads over their friends' kamikaze antics of the previous evening. However, the overpowering and unmistakable smell of silage brought me back to stark reality as the car pulled up beside a shrouded steading and tattie field whose long dreels crawled away towards the sea.

In this "Season Of Mists and Mellow Fruitfulness" and a nip in the air, there is, among elderly ladies, a real sense of nostalgia, and their greeting of "Aye, it's a real tattie morning," makes you feel they are back in the days when Worzel Gummidge was walking out with Aunt Sally. My late, hardy mother's annual tale of these times was how, after a long day at the tattie lifting, she and a crowd of other young folk walked four miles to a dance-

"Where her light feet were never off the floor until two in the morning"-walked home again, and was back on the frosty field for yolkin' time.

We all have our memories, and after my first day at the tatties, I went with all the righteous indignation of a four year old to my father, who was busy dishing out the brown envelopes to all and sundry, and asked why I hadn't got one, because, "I've worked hard all day, my back's sore, my wellies are full of earth and there are thistles in my fingers." Considering that paying me had obviously never entered his head, he put up a good show and said my money was at home, and because I'd made such a lot, he'd been afraid I might lose it in the field!

Bruin One was up at the old homestead for a day or two, and when, surprisingly, we fell to reminiscing about the times she and Bruin Two had spent in the tattie field, she said that he used to keep all the rotten ones he found and fling them at her rear end when no one was looking. She also laughed about the time she helped a friend with his tatties on one of her weekends off, and how, when she returned to her ward the following Monday walking in like a half shut knife, an elderly male patient was horrified to learn where she'd acquired her sore back. "Well, sister," he said indignantly, "I think that's awfy that you've had tae gang oot tae the tatties because your pey's no big enough tae live on."

Now all this happy memories stuff is fine, but with Father Bear away from sunrise to sunset every day I'm back on the pieces again and these days he's away with enough in his outsize piecebox to feed himself and Desperate Dan (I cook cow pie for supper). He says the machine lifts around 13 acres a day, and he and the other men never have a moment to spare as they drive the tattie boxes back and forth. But there'll never be any nostalgia in that will there? Gone are the days of the real, down to earth, backbreaking stuff. The harassed mother whose bairns wouldn't pick their half bit. The cheer which went up when the old digger, which whirled frantically round like a Catherine Wheel, broke down. The jokes, the banter, the songs, the moles, the mice and the bottom line of it all – the money.

* * *

Hip, Hip, Hooray for the Sunshine Harvest

Huggans, pixie pears, chopps, nipper nails and pigs noses ... are you with me? I wouldn't be with me either if I hadn't found out they were the local names given throughout the country to our humble rose-hips whose cheerful August red berries can still be seen clinging to their bare, tossing branches in the snell, snow laden winter winds.

Now, I'm not going to launch into some long winded spiel about them, but it was only very recently I found out that there was much more to these modest little stores of goodness than met the eye. Apparently, in the middle ages, when cultivated fruit was scarce, they were slit open, deseeded, pulped and used to flavour all kinds of sweet meats. During the First World War, it was suggested they could be made into jam, but this was a gey laborious task because they were so small and footery to prepare. During the Second World War, however, when citrus foods were in very short supply, the humble hip was to become a very important source of Vitamin C after it was found to contain four times that of blackcurrants and twenty times that of oranges.

Well, in these far off days of sweetie rationing and Billy and Bunny, our elderly Headmistress, a woman of steel, told us this heart roasting tale about the poor, pale children who lived in cities where the grimy, high buildings and smoke-filled air shut out the sunshine needed to give them this wonderful stuff called Vitamin C. And, she went on, spraying the front desks' occupants with fine spit, you can help them become healthy. We, of course, were complete suckers for this propaganda, and putty in her plump, pink hands. All you have to do, she explained, is pick rose-hips. Eh, what, rose-hips, was that it? Seeing her taskforce sitting silently like a dozen deflated balloons, she went on with renewed vigour to tell us about this rose-hip syrup business and how, as well as helping the poor children (we could picture them standing listless in their gloomy playground, their little furred

tongues begging for a few drops of this magic pink stuff) we would be paid for our efforts. Two dozen ears pricked up instantly and we were back on the glory trail again. By the time she'd finished her rallying speech we were desperate for 3.30 p.m. to arrive so that we could race off and start picking.

The first half-mile of our journey was spent fighting over bushes, nursing scratches, hauling our clothes off trailing barbed brambles and stuffing our bags and pockets with hips. Who said money didn't grow on trees!

We all tore off home in different directions for our tea, and despite my great excitement about our first venture into an industry relying totally on wild hips, picked by folk like us, my reception was decidedly lukewarm. Auntie, (Mother's unmarried sister who lived with us) remarked very sourly - "I'll bet that auld besom'll no be oot pickin' hips onywey, but she's awfy good at gettin' a'body else tae dae her donkey work." Teachers in her opinion led a lady's life. However, one afternoon, when I was at school, she and mother set off with wooden tomato baskets, old coats and shepherds crooks, in a similar fashion to that of the two delightful ladies in the cookery programme, and the fruits of their labour were proudly displayed on the big kitchen table when I arrived home.

Nearly every day (before projects and practical maths) I wobbled off to school with my bicycle basket full of rosy, red hips and over the ensuing weeks we filled, weighed and stacked our sacks which were collected regularly by the "hips man." In every aspect of life though, there is a snag, and ours was a thin, hardworking soul with childlike ways, who'd been boarded out for many years on a local farm, and who, every other day, trudged over the fields with a large sack of predominantly green hips on her poor, stooped back. We did protest, but our parents had told us that her hip money was the only pay she ever saw and so, with our usual token grumbles, we duly allocated and mixed her "greenies" throughout all the bags.

At the end of the season, we tallied up the pounds we'd picked and the money we'd made, and although we heard that a school near Newcastle had picked 30,000lbs, we knew it was only Erchie's bad leg that stood between us and that amount. Then came the grand finale, the three rousing cheers for our efforts, which began with those heartfelt words, "HIP, HIP, HIP HOORAY!"

The Best Laid Plans

I had my first taste of meetings the day Big Tam arrived at school with money his sisters had given him and insisted that he wanted to treat us all to something from the baker's van which usually arrived at going home time. Of course, we all knew his sisters would skin him alive if word of this ever got back to them and so we decided to hold a meeting and draw up a fool proof plan. (We didn't realise there was no such thing.) Anyway, when we were all sitting in the long grass behind the playground dyke wolfing up "sympathetic" cream sponges, fruitcakes, doughnuts and iced cookies, and licking our sticky fingers, we thanked the big fella for his kindness and suggested we could maybe do it again sometime. Tam, who was munching a big daud of fruitcake, nodded affably. When I arrived home I wasn't very hungry, but, by good luck, mother was busy and she didn't notice the cat sitting under the table polishing off most of my tea. Tam, however, was an absolute disaster. The silly fool had apparently run all the way home in case he was late for his tea and vomited this cascade of colourful confectionery all over the doorstep in full view of his mother.

Now, in these far off days of Tam's fall from grace and Lassie's rise to stardom, meetings weren't high on life's agenda. Father never went to any, but he good naturedly drove his car load of "Old Yowes" to the W.R.I. with strict instructions from mother to keep his silly remarks to himself and not give her a showing up. I think I must have taken after his light hearted approach to meetings, because for years I refused to have anything to do with them or committees.

However, the day came when I had neither excuse nor escape from going on the two younger Bruins' Playgroup committee, but the meetings were short and sweet. After all, how long does it take to arrange a sponsored "wheelie" round a wee patch of grass and hand out some biscuits and juice? Ah, but that was only the beginning, and over the years the meetings grew in quantity until the memorable day I was delegated to the dizzy heights of making the tea and coffee at a coffee morning. There I was, like a frazzled ferret, flying about in all the steam whilst kettle lids whistled and danced around me. I bet James Watt was helping out at a coffee morning too, when he first became aware of the potential of steam.

Most of the meetings I became involved in were get togethers to organise local events ranging from bonfire suppers to Tombola stalls at our local Agricultural Show, where elderly country loons smilingly accepted their prizes of Mickey Mouse pencilcases and seven year-old bairns scowled in disgust at their teabags and handcream.

Once the two younger Bruins were house trained and able to tie their shoe-laces, I decided it was time to plough again the set-aside area of my mind, where the seeds of farming folklore had lain dormant for years. In doing so, my scribblings about an embittered, lonely old spinster whose neep shawing days ended when she and a forlorn, tattered tattie-bogle went off like kindred spirits into the Hallowe'en mirk, led me into another field with its own crop of meetings.

If you're familiar with the poem called "The Boy In The Train," you'll know about the endless questions he asked on his first rail journey to Kirkcaldy. Well, when I was at a meeting in The Lang Toon and a knowledgeable elderly gentleman who was pouring over the menu said, "I don't know what I'll have for my tea to-night?" it seemed a perfect time and place to enquire, "A herrin' or maybe a haddie?" "No," came his totally humourless reply, "We'd fish last night, I think I'll settle for the ham salad." Ach well, somebody's got to be serious in this world.

Deep down I'm not really your sophisticated meetings type, because I find all those pages of apologies, minutes, sub-committees, and A.O.C.B.'s gey tedious, and my nodding off doesn't exactly endear me to folk who've spent weeks on their speeches. Secretly, it's always been my great wish to get up and give Gene Kelly's song and dance routine from "Singing In The Rain" laldy, but I suppose it would simply be minuted as "Matters Arising From The Floor!"

Say Cheese.....or Potato

Well, they're back! I knew as soon as I heard the gnawing and scuttling noises coming from within the walls, and saw the "tell-tail" tiny bomb shaped droppings in the cupboard that the little varmits had arrived for their all-inclusive winter holiday package. Although I didn't see it, I could just picture the wee, double decker bus full of little suitcases, holdalls and excited passengers squealing with delight at the prospect of exploring all the nooks and crannies of their "Full Board, Five-Star Hotel."

Now, they've had a bonus this year, because, our faithful, endearing mousekeeper with the racoon strippit tail passed on in September, and lies buried under a honeysuckle bush in a sunny, sheltered corner of the garden. But before cats with references start arriving by the van load, let me assure you that things are not so serious as they might seem, because we have another skilled mouser in the person of Grandfather Bear, a man outstanding in his field, who has polished off more mice and moles than Desperate Dan (whose demise could have worsened an industry already beleaguered with problems) has had cow pies.

"I'll need a bitty cheese," said the maestro, as he sat with his specs on, fiddling about with two rusty mouse traps which had seen better days. "Will I go and buy some more traps?" I asked. "Na, na, they'll dae fine," was the confident reply. I was a bit worried about his fingers, but no, all was well, and the traps were duly loaded and set in the dishes press and the glory-hole under the stairs. The first big 'SNAP' came just after teatime, and the sound of clattering metal was music to the ears of the triumphant trapper who emerged gleefully from the press, brandishing a mouse the size of a horse. In order that familiarity would not breed contempt, morsels of raw tattie were substituted for cheese, and within a few days, several of the holiday revellers had had their chips.

You know, when you think about it, who decided that eight out of ten mice prefer cheese anyway? Have the furries ever actually come out and said so? I bet they all gather at nights to share out their little Happy Meal carryouts, and find to their dismay that they've all got cheese. My mother once made a cheese but we were all so anxious to taste it that it was finished before it had time to mature. She made butter every week, and one morning when she went to collect her big basin of cream from what we called the dairy, she found a great fat mouse had abseiled right into it. Our pig must have thought it was his birthday as he slurped up his breakfast of tatties and cream. One of my auntie's left a big tin of home made treacle toffee to set over night, and the following morning, much to her disgust and dismay, she found a mouse embedded up to his orchestras (as the youngest Bruin used to call them) in the solidified stuff.

Talking of the youngest Bruin brings to mind the day he fished his new football boots out of the glory-hole and found one of them had been chewed to bits by mice. Nowadays, he can see the funny side of the tragedy which he refers to as "Moose In Boots," but it was enough to make Gazza greet into his crisps at the time.

It was around this time of year that Robert Burns wrote his famous poem in which he described so vividly his feelings for the poor mouse he'd rendered homeless when his plough cut though its little dwelling. I used to feel very sorry for the legions of shivering little brown families too, who fled in terror on a threshing mill day, when the bottom stooks in which they'd made their winter's abode were forked off to feed the ever hungry mill.

However, the present only touches me, and before my space runs out, I must tell you about the coat. Every time Grandfather Bear catches another mouse or mole I ask how many more he'll need to finish my fabulous and unique fur coat. It will have a ratio of two mouse pelts to every mole, it will be cut on the bias so that it will have a swing to it, it will be ankle-length and it will be the talk of the supermarket. (Steamies have gone). So if you see a big wummin in size eight boots wearing a coat of this description, scuttling around with a trolley load of cheese, you'll know it's me.

Fare To Tickle The Taste Buds

I bought a beautifully illustrated, top of the range, glossy Christmas magazine yesterday which showed me how, step by step, I could achieve everything from looking absolutely fabulous to decorating the mantlepiece with foliage high enough to topple half the horses in the Grand National. When I showed Father Bear and the youngest Bruin the pictures of the brandied, prune ice-cream (prunes smack of Syrup of Figs) and turkey and stilton patties served in rocket leaves, garnished with chopped red onions, their comments weren't really printable. In all fairness, however, I have to admit that such sophisticated works of nouvelle cuisine are a far cry, too, from the humble Christmas fare my mother prepared for us when I was a little girl, and when I found a quote in the magazine saying "Childhood Christmases are the ones we most fondly remember" my mind began to drift back down the years.

The rich, warm, spicy smell of mother's fruitcakes, blackbuns and mince-pies baking in the rayburn permeated the whole house for days, and she used to sit with a hairnet on de-seeding muscatel raisins in front of a candle flame, in case there was the slightest hint of a 'crunch' in any of her masterpieces. In the week leading up to Christmas she and auntie would be found sitting red nosed in the cold stick-shed, up to their ears in feathers, as they stoically plucked their way through all the cockerels which had been reared for folks' festive dinners.

After all the birds, the baking, the hand knitted socks, the ounces of tobacco and the braces of pheasants (poached unashamedly by father, who insisted he'd fed the beggars all year) had been despatched by bus to previously notified relatives, I knew it was nearly time for Santa to arrive.

One year father came home from the market and declared that he'd seen "Auld Clauser" having a dram or two, but then, of course, in these distant days of woolly vests and the McFlannels, there was no such thing as the breathalyser. I used to lie in my moonlit bedroom under the eaves of the creaking old house and picture this trail of shimmering stars swishing silently through the velvet night and, as I strained to catch the first faint tinkling of the golden sleigh bells, I hoped that the silly old goat didn't go Ho! Ho! Ho! and drop off another bloomin' sledge, because I didn't want the first one he brought (I'd a perfectly good big tin milk basin) let alone the second one, and where was the doll's pram I'd asked for to hurl my cats around in? Mother always said folk got fair fuddled with drink! I usually received a good present from Santa when he came to the school party, but then, I'd told the 'Mother Hen' the saga of the sledges because I knew she wouldn't stand for any of his drunken nonsense.

At that time, Christmas was still a working day, and when our cheery rosy-faced postie arrived on his bike, he was welcomed with a thick slice of iced Christmas cake and a dram. He always brought us a thank you present for the "lifesaving" cups of tea and bits of homebaking that mother gave him on his twenty mile round, up hill and downdale trip.

The first course of our eagerly awaited traditional dinner on the big table in the warm, stone flagged, lamp lit kitchen was tomato soup, and that was followed by a huge roasted cockerel with oatmeal, suet and onion stuffing, roast potatoes, mashed potatoes and turnip, and if we had any room left, there was Christmas pudding and cream.

Right, that's my nostalgia trip over and now, I'm just dying to tell you about the very exciting pre-Christmas, gift bearing journey we had last weekend, when we travelled afar to see a new and very special baby girl. Bruin Two and his wife, a kind and gentle lass who will make a lovely mum, made us grandparents and aunties and uncles and things for the very first time, and we're all tickled pink.

I wonder if the Three Kings thought long and hard about what to take to their new baby? No doubt if they were alive today and were anything like Father Bear, they'd send 'the wife' down to the old bazaar for some 'Posh Spice' or a set of Teletubbies.

* * *

You'd Better Watch Out For The Troll Patrol!

The back door of the farmhouse crashes open at day-break on New Year's morning and in stumbles the Good Man, reeking of drink, covered in gutters and full of the joys of life. His Good Lady, whose tongue has been simmering on the hob all night, launches into a scalding attack on him and demands to know where he's been 'til this hour? "Where have I been?" he repeats slowly, with all the politeness of the paralytic. "I've been and falling in with a crowd of Trolls." "Oh, Trolls, that explains everything then," says the Good Lady sarcastically, "and wha are they when they're at hame?" "Well," he says, waving his arms about, "they're big, ugly, goblin like craiturs." "Is that so, well it's no hard tae work oot the craitur you've been gobblin," she comments sourly. "No, no," insists the Good Man, "as sure as I stand here in this kitchen, I swear's true, and do you know this? You're lucky to see me, for they wanted to take me away for a year." "A year," she repeats, "they'd be back wie ye efter twa days."

Unlikely though it may seem, he could well have been telling the truth, because Hogmanay was the one night in the year when the troublesome Trolls could leave their dark, cavernous homes deep inside the mountains and come and wreak havoc and mischief on the surrounding countryside and its inhabitants. Now, the Trolls were bad enough, but alas, they weren't the only unwelcome revellers around, for it was also the night when witches, 'wee folk', ghosts and everything else from the world of folklore and legend were free to roam the earth. It was small wonder, then, that in those dark days when superstitions ran high, frightened families brought an assortment of branches and greenery into their homes to safeguard themselves from impending evil. Rowan above the door was supposed to bring luck, holly kept the fairies away, and the magic powers of hazel and yew protected all who dwelt within.

I can understand how these poor souls felt, because one Hogmanay the Snook arrived in our house and it lurked in the dark, flickering firelight of the best bedroom. Its evil presence terrified me and the very mention of its name sent me scuttling down the dark, creaking staircase to the safety of the friendly kitchen where I arrived with goose fleshy arms and a thumping heart. Years later, when I was ten, I came face to face with the dreaded thing and found, much to my humiliation, that it was no more than the discarded, snooty piece of a man's bonnet one of my female relatives had tried to remodel into a hat, in those thrifty days of make do and mend. Being the youngest of about a hundred cousins often had its drawbacks!

I loved the last, bustling days of the outgoing year when the old house was cleaned and polished until it shone (it was considered bad luck to enter a New Year with anything less), and the visitors' rooms smelled cosy and warm with their sparking log fires, which often set our hearth hugging, much singed, old grey cat alight yet again.

Our poor pig always died with the year, and if he wasn't around in spirit, he was there in body, because we used every bit of him like the Plains' Indians did with the buffalo. Mother usually made potted meat, but I thought it was awful shivery kind of stuff and I used to squelch it around in my mouth until it had heated up a bit.

Mother got pretty heated up too, when she heard through Cock Robin (a clyping little beggar of a bird who should have had his tongue cut out) that I'd told several ladies at the school Christmas party "Mummy's getting lots of visitors on Hogmanay and she doesn't want them."

I looked forward to having visitors, because apart from being friendly and cheerful, they always brought bags full of wonderful goodies which I seldom saw, and I felt the old house, too, became alive with the warmth and laughter of their presence.

Well, all this talk about cleaning old houses and having visitors is a timely reminder that I'd better get tore in to our ancestral pile with the vacuum cleaner and a tin of polish, because I could write my name in the stoor, and Hogmanay's only two days away. But, before I do, my wish for you all in 1998 is "That the moose ne'er leave your mealpoke wi' a teardrop in its e'e." Oh, and a word   of warning ..... Watch out for the Troll Patrol.

Early Taste of a Grand Tradition

"A blast o' Janwar' win' blew" me in on the annual Burns Supper in our little country hall when I wasn't much bigger than a Teletubby (I'd probably have been Laa Laa) and as I sat there, on my best behaviour, in front of a crisply starched tablecloth weighed down by heavy cutlery waiting for the action to begin, I tried to make some sense of it all.

Now, I knew Robert Burns had written poems about mice and things, but why had everyone come to his birthday supper when he'd been dead even longer than our dog? There was a photo of him hanging on the wall, but, he looked awful well dressed to be a farmer, and he seemed even more in need of a haircut than father who'd been nagged at all week to go to the barber. "Look," he said to Mother, "It's far ower cauld the noo and ye ken fine a' the weemin'll be after me if I'm ower guid lookin'."

Suddenly, after a lot of kerfuffle, the stiff kitchen door burst open and from a cloud of squealing and droning steam, a piper emerged, followed by three harassed, red-faced ladies looking ladies carrying large ashets of food which they laid ceremoniously in front of the important people at the top table. (Everyone stood for this procession and it was all I could do not to burst out laughing, but, in the nick of time, I remembered Mother's strict Burns Supper code of etiquette). Well, no sooner was the haggis laid down in front of this awful enthusiastic looking mannie than he began to say things about it . Then he stabbed its poor glossy hurdies with a great big knife until thick, brown, porridge looking stuff came oozing out of the deep wound. As soon as this ritual was over, half a dozen ladies came racing round with plates of haggis, neeps and tatties on trays and a silence fell on the place as we all stuck in to our "bill o' fare".

Everyone ate "Till a' their weel swall'd kytes belyve were bent like drums" and then we had the toast. Now this toast was a funny business, because it wasn't a toast at all, it was a dram (only my dram was lemonade) and every wee while we stood up and a said a toast to other folk who didn't appear to be there either. But that's grown-ups for you.

After that, things became more and more boring and I couldn't honestly say "The minutes winged their way wi' pleasure" as men droned on about the things this poet had got up to, and the grown-ups laughed knowingly at jokes I didn't think were funny at all. Worse was to come, however, after a big lady with a white blouse and a very fat kilt was helped on to the stage. "Wi' mony an eldritch skreech" she battled her way through "Ca' The Yowes Tae The Knowes" and "Comin' Through The Rye". She was followed by a little man who poured his heart and soul into "Ae Fond Kiss" and "My Luve Is Like A Red, Red Rose." The man beside me must have enjoyed it though, because he whispered to the lady sitting next to him "That it was enough tae bring the tears tae a gless ee'."

Three years later I was just about in tears too, when the 'Mother Hen' decided that I should sing two songs at the Bard's forthcoming 'do' because I had a "nice little voice". On the dreaded night, the mouse wasn't the only one with "a panic in its breastie." My thin, bony little knees were going like castanets as I stood waiting to make my big debut in front of all those expectant, and in two cases, critical faces. What made matters worse was the songs which had been chosen for me .... 'Scotswahay' (I thought it was somebody's name) and 'Willie Wastle's Wife'. Apart from not knowing what half the words in 'Scots Wha Hae' meant, the big boys in the school kept singing a rude version (it was very funny) which I was terrified of lapsing into. As for the second song, what ever possessed him to pick her in the first place?

And that, as all the good fairy stories say, is how it all began. Down the years I've dragged a sledge laden with mashed tatties, neeps and dumpling across the frozen snows of January, I've sung at many suppers, and I've read widely of the Bard whose most famous quote of all "That man tae man the world o'er, shall brothers be for a' that" is just as fervent a hope for mankind today as it was when he died in 1796 at the age of 37.

Not Simply Idle Moaners

Last week a gentleman put the following question to me ... "Do Farmers Deserve To Be Classed As A Bunch Of Moaners?" with the emphasis on the word "Deserve." Now, what with Father Bear having only that day been complaining bitterly about tasteless bloomin' plastic chips (the handy oven variety), working boots that only lasted five minutes, dreich weather and the new cat glowerin' at him, I thought 'Moaning, I'm married to a guy with a First Class Honours Degree in it!' However, as the question was set at a deeper level than the squad of moles who're busy landscaping the big field, I knew answering it wouldn't be an easy task. I also decided not to enter into politics and policies because I wouldn't know where to begin and anyway, it's not my intention to get folks' galluses in a twist early in the morning when they could well be heading for 'One Of Those Days.'

Talking of days, let's look at a pretty typical one here. The postie arrives early with a bundle of mail, which is full of useless circulars, buff envelopes and letters from the Queen. Minutes later there's a lot of ripping and swearing coming from the office, an impressive title for an untidy, paper strewn wee room sporting a sofa which has been vandalised by an over enthusiastic cat. Father Bear emerges in a cloud of cigarette smoke and mutters that he's off to get the tractor yolkit. To what, is anybody's guess. Half an hour later he's back looking like a greased monkey; it won't start and there's a puddle of oil lying under it. (It's not my fault, like, but I'm the nearest pair of ears). He then 'phones the hard pressed mechanic, who, by the sound of things, can't come until teatime, or even tomorrow. Then the 'phone rings, it's a neighbour with the glad tidings that one of the horse lodgers has decided the grass is definitely greener on the other side of the fence so he's jumped into the adjoining field of oilseed rape. Meanwhile, a pleasant old country mannie arrives in his car wondering if he can get a couple of bags of dung for his garden. Realising that, like The Ancient Mariner, he's found a sympathetic ear, Father Bear spends half an hour chatting to the old fellow, who putters off in his car half an hour later, shaking his head as he goes home to tell the wife that he "disna envy fermers nooadays."

Why is farm life governed by Sod's Law? Why is there never such a thing as a normal, predictable, trouble free working day? Why is there a band of cattle running about on the road at 1.30 a.m. on a pouring wet Sunday morning when folk have just returned from their first night out in months? Why do accidents never happen at quiet times? Why does the smart seven year old who spends every spare minute in the cab become allergic to work when he's 17? And why does an elderly, male relative never fail to turn up at your elbow at the height of every crisis with his prophetic phase - "I kent fine that wid happen." Aggravating though it may be, he's usually right, for he's seen it before. He's lived through the good and the bad times. He's worked out in all weathers and he's practically waterproof. Would he do it again? "Na. If I'd my life tae live again ye widnae catch me on a ferm, ye're far better aff wie a job. Ye've nae worries."

But you try telling most folk that. The general impression is, and always has been, that farmers are a bunch of greetin faced, well heeled, want for nothing, driving around in a top of the range vehicle fat cats, who wouldn't know what hardship meant even if they met it in their big plates of home made broth, steak pie and steam pudding and custard. Sadly though, for every fat cat, there are many thin and disillusioned cats, struggling to exist in circumstances which have spiralled out of their control. So, "Do Farmers Deserve To Be Classed As A Bunch Of Moaners?" I don't think they do, it's just as the old farmer said, "But I'm no moanin' lassie, I'm jist tellin' ye whit happened."

Will it be the same in 100 years' time? Who knows. I'll leave you to reflect on these two verses which were written in the 1880s.

Nae won'er tho' the times mak's us a' discontented
For faith the puir farmers they've cause tae complain;
The meal is cheap sellin', their fairms high rentit,
And sma' is their profit when sellin' their grain.

Some one thing, some other, likewise the bad weather,
The craps torn doon wi' the torrents o' rain.
The cattle that's parket will no tak' the market.
We'll jis tak' them in a twalmonth again.

When Budding Rock Stars "Music" Boomed Around

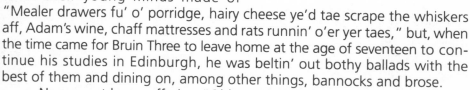

When the two younger Bruins were just wee lads pedalling around on their sturdy little blue and red tractors, Grandfather Bear used to take a delight in telling them what their life would be like "When they left hame and went tae live in the bothy." Now, I really don't know what their young minds made of "Mealer drawers fu' o' porridge, hairy cheese ye'd tae scrape the whiskers aff, Adam's wine, chaff mattresses and rats runnin' o'er yer taes," but, when the time came for Bruin Three to leave home at the age of seventeen to continue his studies in Edinburgh, he was beltin' out bothy ballads with the best of them and dining on, among other things, bannocks and brose.

Now, most long suffering "Old Foggies" will assure you the brighter side of the young Bruins leaving home is that you will gain a bedroom, stand a better chance of getting into the bathroom, and get rid of the deafening chart toppers, which will for years have caused your walls and windows to dirl and your cat to seek refuge on the fork lift seat. Well (and I say this without boasting) Father Bear and I can go one better. We had a real, live "Heavy Metal" band at our little house on the prairie, when Bruin Two, who, in those days lived to play the guitar (and who now plays the guitar to live) set up his 'jamming sessions' in an old wooden shed right next to the living room window. Nearly every evening an old banger full of budding rock stars, guitars, drums and enough flex for an open air concert in Hyde Park came stooring into the close, and about an hour later their electric guitars could be heard twanging into action and their relentless drums sounded like those of the Sioux about to go on the warpath. The noise was completely off the Richter scale and it could be heard for miles around in the soft, summer twilight. What our shed of brown laying hens thought of the din can only be imagined, but, the 'band' delighted in telling folk that it was quite usual for them to play for an audience of 5000. They once persuaded Father Bear to act as their 'Roadie' and take them to a talent competition in a distant mining town, where their act went down like a lump of frozen dumpling among tartan 'go go' dancers and sweet singers. When he was asked if he "kent whaur that awfy racket were frae?" (I've had to miss out a few choice adjectives here) he denied all knowledge of them and slunk outside to sit in the van.

These were busy days, but looking back, they were happy days. Bruin One's friends joined in all the action and we were never short of helpers to gather, grade and sell our mountains of brown eggs and entertain the two little Bruins, who were at that stage when it seemed perfectly normal to have a house bursting at the seams with people, and a noisy band in the shed. At nights our small kitchen was filled with cheery young folk singing and joking as they wired into hot buttered toast liberally spread with strawberry jam, and drank gallons of tea.

"Time" however, as the old song goes "brings a'thing tae an end," and so the two older Bruins, like the swallows, left home at the end of that summer and went their separate ways. They were sadly missed, and their rooms, so unnaturally tidy, were now silent and still. I thought about them constantly. What would they be having for their tea? Would they remember to dry their clothes properly? Were they happy? Did they miss us? When would we see them again? Would they manage to cope with their new life?

Of course they managed. We managed didn't we, and even if we hadn't, would we have admitted it?

I've been down this road three times now, and does it get any easier? No, not really, but you just have to accept it and hope that life will be kind to them.

They've all returned many, many times over the years, and as Bruin Four said recently, when he heard his sister was getting married in July, "Oh, good, we're getting another member of the family." And what about him? Is he leaving home? Nae Fears, he's bidin' here. He reckons that, apart from a "couple of drawbacks," hame's no a bad place.

Left Powerless – And Not Even A Coal Fire To Warm Us Up

Father Bear was watching television, the two young Bruins were at a friend's 21st birthday party and I was lying fine and cosy in bed enjoying a rare, late night cup of tea and a piece of cake and listening to the howling wind splattering snow flakes against the window. Ah, this is the life, I thought, as I put down the magazine I'd been reading, I bet I'll go out like a light tonight. Well, before a mouse had time to sneeze, the room was plunged into darkness; the elderly radio alarm gave a little peep, the radiator gurgled apologetically, and a deafening silence descended upon the whole house. Oh blast, I fumed, is that not bloomin' typical. I lay there expecting to hear Father Bear crashing about downstairs among the furniture and shouting "What's happened to the lights?" (I'm supposed to know all these things). But there wasn't a sound. I'll bet he's fallen asleep, I thought, as I crept cautiously down to the living room hoping I wouldn't trip over Buffy the cat who would no doubt be around somewhere. I managed to find my two candlesticks with their long, tapered candles and as I fumbled around for matches, I could feel a chill spreading through the house. When the tiny flames grew taller I located Father Bear, whose first question on being awakened was. "Have you phoned the Electricity Board?" and his next, "What did they say?" I plonked a candle down in front of him, told him to phone them himself and reminded him he'd to collect the Bruins, before I shot back upstairs to a frozen bed. The three of them clattered in about twenty minutes later, full of good spirits and witty suggestions as to how they could best share two candles among three people and singing 'Wee Willie Winkie.'

When I woke in the morning, the room was bathed in snowy daylight, but the blank look on the face of the alarm reminded me that the power was still off. "We'll just let sleeping bears lie," I said to Buffy who plodded heavily down in front of me to the polar regions below, "they'll only moan anyway." Now, if we were sensible folk, we'd have some contingency plan or other drawn up for power cuts, but what have we got .... a few candles and a generator that takes about half a day to wire up. In the not too distant past, when we had broiler chickens, this same generator roared into life the minute the power in their sheds went off, but it goes without saying, of course, that we still had to guddle about with dribbly candles in the house until such time as we were thrown a light line. At least we had a coal fire in those good old days.

Anyway, our present problem wasn't going to be alleviated by reminiscing and as I struggled into my second coat, a shivering Father Bear joined me and suggested that I should phone a friend a couple of miles away and ask if she would fill our flasks with boiling water (he's a stickler for traditional values, and knows that from time immemorial it's been the woman's job to be the water carrier)! Now, if he'd thought this one through, he'd have gone himself, because not only did our friend very kindly fill our flasks, she also sat me down beside a wonderful coal fire, where we newsed over tea and biscuits, and it was only a feeling of guilt that drove me back to Bleak House nearly an hour later bearing flasks and further offers of help.

Once the excitement of the first cup of hot tea abated, the three of them prowled about the house like something in a small enclosure at the zoo. Board games were suggested "Board games! We're bored, nae desperate." "What's for the dinner?" "Rolls and ham." "Fried Ham?" "How could it be fried ham?" "Aw, it's no that shivery stuff wi' rabbits food is it?" "What about a bar lunch?" "No, we'll have a take-a-way at tea time." Between clenched teeth I sat there and quoted one of Burns' most famous lines "O wad some power the Giftie gie us" and he did. A wee while later, after fourteen long hours, our power was restored by an unseen, but much appreciated band of hardy lads, and our home became alive with the sound of music once more.

* * *

Signs Of Spring, But Is Winter Really Far Behind?

"Cauld Winter it is noo awa, and Spring has come again;

And the cauld dry winds o' March month hae driven awa the rain.

Hae driven awa the dreary rain likewise the frost and snaw;

So our foreman in the mornin' he's ordered out tae saw."

I can mind the days of pixie hoods and hairy tweed coats with government health warnings, when we had winters like that, and how the grown-ups used to look forward to the "bonnie spring days" when the warming wind would blow across the braes and go off arm in arm with the last of the winter's snow. I can also remember very vividly, and I probably shouldn't tell you this, of a not so distant spell of hard weather, when I was in bed with a humdinger of a sore throat and unable to wash the two younger Bruins' school clothes. I gave Father Bear instructions on how to work the washing machine and off he went. Well, when I saw the results I was in tears. Somehow or other, he'd set the bloomin' thing at the very hottest wash (he still blames me for duff instructions) and everything had shrunk so much that the two of them wouldn't have looked out of place in Fagin's den or Oliver Twist's workhouse).

But, seriously, what's happened to this "For everything there is a season" business? I know we're only a few days away from March, but we've had leaves on our rhubarb since the second week in February, the oilseed rape doesn't know whether it's coming or going, the daffies are a foot high and I told Grandfather Bear that he was just showing off when I saw he had roses blooming in his garden. Are we tempting providence by thinking we're into spring when we've never really had a winter? Only time will tell, but Grandfather Bear assures us that the great snow storm of 1947 didn't start until "March month."

Anyway, with the possibility that Spring really could be here, is Father Bear sawin' yet? Na, he's getherin' stanes. "They're steens, nae stanes" says Bruin Three, our 'orra' student of Doric and dialects, who dropped in for a couple of days on his way north to a big bothy ballad 'Do' and found himself conscripted into the 'steen squad' before he'd even had time to remove his jacket.

The following morning while the wild geese were still clanking around the loch discussing their day's route, 'Fred' and 'Barney' Bruin set off with the others on the tractor and bogey and digger bound for 'Bedrock', and I must admit, they were more cheerful than I'd expected them to be as they went out the door singing and joking in their old green boiler suits and oil stained boots. On their return, hours later, they were like clay cats, but still quite cheerful, and "hungry enough to eat a scabbie horse 'atween twa mattresses." Now, I could be wrong but, at the back of my mind, I've always had a sneaking suspicion that Father Bear actually enjoys seeing the young Bruins "getherin steens," because, you see, when he was a young Bruin (in the days when Black Bob was the only version of One Man And His Dog) he "aye had tae pick steens on his Easter holidays." And so, it is also my belief (though I know he'll deny it) that even if we didn't have a stone about the place, he'd bring a few loads in just for the sheer hell of it.

It has often been said too, that in Spring a young man's thoughts turn to love, and we were all delighted recently when a very pleasant young man proposed to Bruin One. Her ring, which has a most unusual "steen" in it, was the subject of all the usual comments you'd expect from a male household ... "How did ye no tell us that ye were needin' a bit o' gless for a ring, there's a bucket of the stuff round in the shed," and "We could've got you a bigger bit than that," and so on. But she knows fine what they're like and reckons that the cheek and banter and tricks she's had to put up with over the years has sharpened her wit and rendered her almost immune to embarrassment.

So, as you will appreciate, I'm up to my neck in wedding plans, and Father Bear, helpful as ever at times like this, said he could quite easily clean out the big shed for the occasion, Grandfather Bear predictably stated that "Brose wid dae folk fine" and Bruin One, what's she saying to all this - "You know, I think 'We Plough The Fields And Scatter' would be a good hymn, don't you?"

* * *

The Much-Maligned Moggie, Unsung Friend Of The Farm

Around most steadings there lurks a core of hardy workers, who, although they are seldom given much recognition for their services, do a grand job nevertheless. By now, the two young Bruins will be preening themselves and thinking "she obviously means us," but, I'm sorry lads, today it's the turn of the humble farm cat.

I've always had a real soft spot for these unsophisticated moggies, because, when I was little (in the days of Roy Rogers and Trigger) our assorted furries were my only pals. I was never a 'dog' person, but maybe that was because Moss, our collie, obviously had what we would nowadays call a 'behaviour problem' ... he bit children, and as I was a right wee feartie, I never went near him. Anyway, me and 'mogs' got along fine; we rambled through the fields, we played at housies, we sledged down the steep, snowy braes and although we didn't speak the same language, the four of us seemed to be on the same wavelength.

When I was around nine, I begged mother to teach me how to milk our cow (I must have been a few sandwiches short of a picnic in these days) and I used to squirt the assembled 'band' with the warm, white liquid they were sitting so patiently waiting for. (I've always felt a bit guilty about that). However, by the time they'd licked all the dribbles of milk off each others faces and whiskers, I'd finished my task, and they purred forgivingly around my legs as we all headed towards their big dish.

Now, every so often in life a real character of a cat will come along and in our case it was Angus. When we went to live in our little house on the prairie, surrounded by red hens (not Indians) we found we'd inherited nine cats ranging from humphy backit wee craturs, to one massive big fella whom we christened Moonface. In all fairness, they were a pretty self sufficient lot who slurped up every broken egg in sight, ate anything we gave them (even runner beans) and kept us in a vermin free zone. So, what about this Angus I mentioned earlier, when did he enter the picture? Well, one day Father Bear came into the house carrying a big black and white kitten. "Who's he?" I enquired, "Oh," said St. Francis, "this is our new, special cat." "What do you mean special cat?" I said sarcastically. "Has it escaped your notice that we already have enough cats to kit out half the county?" "Well," came the reply, "the poor devil's been shut in the neighbour's hen shed for a while and I took pity on him." The brutal truth, when it emerged, was that this beast had been banished from house to hen shed for ripping up the folks' upholstery and furniture.

Anyway, our offender was given his chance of rehabilitation and soon it became obvious that his hilarious antics well outweighed his antisocial tendencies. Oh, he had a whale of a time. He demolished Christmas trees, swung like a monkey through clothes horses hanging with wet washing, pounced on folks' bare feet, dived around under the bedclothes, had wrestling matches with Father Bear, who chauffeured him round the countryside before Postman Pat and Jesse had hit Greendale, and he ate poor Reggie, the canary who'd been booked in for a little holiday in the country. Over the years he became a mini-celebrity and he accepted holiday postcards and health enquiries with his usual aplomb.

Time and tide, however, wait for neither man nor cat, and one sad day Angus was laid to rest in his favourite corner of the garden where, a year later, he was joined by his pleasant, but very ordinary, wee strippit friend.

After our hankies had dried, we went to the nearby cat shelter where we were introduced to 'Her Ladyship', a huge twelve year old, foxy coloured tabby of immense proportions, who glowered disdainfully at the approaching riff raff. We were awash with pity when we heard of the death of her elderly mistress and the need for a country home where she could continue in the hunt and other activites of that ilk.

At first she was to be called Clarissa but, in view of the cat shelter's proximity to a very royal home, we felt 'Buffy' was just what one would have chosen. And, how is she doing? Well, her tummy sags, she's awful short of teeth, she's very timid, she's too fat to catch a mouse under the old dresser and she's become my shadow, but then, as Father Bear so delicately pointed out, (after she'd constantly given his friendly "Who's a nice pussycat then," the brush off), "She's just an auld wifie's cat."

* * *

No Smoke Without Fire At Spring Cleaning Time

When I was young (in the days when folk ate plain bread) Spring cleaning was one of life's annual upheavals which drove women to feats of superhuman strength and men to despair. Life, for a few weeks was ruled by "The Cleanin" and wherever women gathered it was their main topic of conversation. Mother and Auntie were, of course, no exception as they humphed mattresses and furniture into the garden, washed blankets, beat the poor rugs until they gasped for mercy and polished everything with the polish advertised by a mouse, standing on a gleaming floor saying, "I can see cousin Willie in Australia." I didn't mind the stuff going into the garden, but when the kitchen and what we called the dairy, were being cleaned out, life was just a total mess. Our big kitchen table disappeared under thousands of clean jam jars, piles of crockery, baking tins, pots, bowls, flat irons and many other things which only saw the light of day once a year. The whole place reeked of wet newspapers and distemper (not the dogs illness, but the forerunner of emulsion paint) and our usual appetising three course meal deteriorated into blubbery boiling beef and tatties.

Now, in case you're thinking that I'm about to bore you to tears telling you how many spiders I've rendered homeless over the past week or two, I'm not. I haven't done any spring cleaning at all, BUT, I know a man who has. Once Father Bear had all his grain sown, he decided that "Things were needin a good reddin' up" and so, first thing next morning, he and Bruin Four (The Fitba' Loon) disappeared round the side of the steading. Soon I could hear the loader moving backwards and forwards followed by the muffled clattering of solid stuff being dropped into a bogey, and when I drove past later on my way to the shops, I got frantic smoking signals to bring cigarettes. (He's like a bear with a burnt tail when he doesn't have any). When I returned with the shopping and the 20 king size, the place looked like a demolition site, but bearing in mind that 'fools and bairns should never see half finished things' I said nothing. Well, the day wore on, the pieces were eaten on the hoof, the conversation, or what there was of it, consisted of words like dump, coup, quarry, weigh-bridge, scrappy and pound notes, or rather, lack of them. After tea Father Bear fell asleep in his chair and the Fitba Loon shot off like a scalded cat to a pal's house. The week slipped by and the noises and the conversation changed little. However, on Saturday morning The Fitba' Loon announced that he was going to a match. "And where's your game today?" enquired Father Bear. "Motherwell" was the reply "MOTHERWELL! So what time are you leaving then?" "I get the supporters bus at half past eleven."

As the second week progressed their enthusiasm began to wane, and progress was slow as the flagging pair tried to sort out all the junk inside the steading. They worked on the principal that if a thing was broken, or hadn't been used since the Second World War (or even both) then it got the heave. Folk round about seeing all the comings and goings must have thought we were leaving, or at least having a roup. Frankly, a roup would probably have been a good idea, because there's always somebody willing to buy rubbish in the fond hope that "It micht come in handy someday!"

Father Bear's Spring cleaning ended, as many noteworthy events do, with a spectacular bonfire which he decided to hold under the cover of darkness. However, Sod's Law stepped in as usual and as the gentle breeze climbed rapidly up the Beaufort Scale, the thick smoke turned and headed towards the main road. The Fitba' Loon was standing with a roasted face and a frozen back when the Boys in Blue appeared and made their enquiries. "Och, it's jist a load of old rubbish and stuff we've been tidying out of the sheds" he replied without enthusiasm. They drove off quite satisfied that there was no cause for alarm.

What really annoys me most about all this tidying up is that I still have bits of machinery with flexes and dials and switches sitting about the house. But he's been warned; one of these days I'm going to throw my rubbish into his tractor and combine cabs and see how he likes it!

* * *

Old Dogs And New

"A bonnie wee gairden fu' o' floors, a kitchen plot an' a'
Wi' carrots and neeps, ingins and leeks, sproots, celery, beans an' beets.
Cabbages, broccoli, lettuces a,' growin', in bonnie wee raws."

That's a great little chorus, isn't it? On my travels through life I haven't come across many farmers who're really into that kind of gardening, but maybe it has something to do with the fact that most farm gardens, including our own, are about the size of a football pitch. My father detested gardening, and his casual "If in doubt, throw it out" attitude resulted in half the flowers blooming cheerfully on the dump, and sheep "keeping down the grass" under the plum trees. Now, after Father Bear and I were married, it soon became evident that like mother, I too had pulled the short straw as far as gardening men go (although I have to be fair here and say that 22 years later he's beginning to show signs of improvement).

Anyway, in our early days among the little red hens, he planted hundreds of cabbages. "You see, if all the folk who come for eggs buy a cabbage too, we'll do quite well." Now, as a result of his constant attention, they were a credit to him, but they were also a total financial flop, because that year, due to Sod's Law, the customers didn't want cabbage, they wanted tatties. Well, after further experiences of 'ingins' which rotted away, mildewed blackcurrants and plagues of greenflee, he more or less threw in the trowel and left gardening alone, until we moved up here, and experienced the full force of the westerly gales.

"I'm going to buy some quick growing trees to shelter us from that wind" he said, and so he planted poplar trees right round the exposed side of the garden. "These trees are growin' at some speed," he remarked some time later. "How tall do they grow?" "Anything up to sixty feet with millions of leaves" I replied. "Aw, ye're jokin" (I'm now writing a new fairy tale called 'Father Bear and The Beanstalks'.)

I thought we'd struck it really lucky when Bruin 3 - (The Bothy Loon) and Bruin 4 - (The Fitba' Loon) were in their early teens, because, suddenly (and before the Hit Squad arrived on screen) gardening became the most important thing in their lives. They spent their pocket money on packets of seed, grow bags and other gardening requisites, and Grandfather Bear, a man whose fingers are greener than the grass, treated them to a fine greenhouse. By Summer, they'd painted it white to protect their plants from the harsh glare of the sun, and it was full of tomatoes and geraniums, and all sorts of other things, which they'd grown from seed. One day, Father Bear accidently tripped and fell through the glass and when I broke the news to the ashen faced Bruins their trembling lips could barely form the question. "Are our tomatoes all right?" In the big vegetable patch they worked equally hard and you could see the two dark heads bobbing about above the dyke as they tilled and toiled and sowed and hoed. After a spell of intensive activity, however, The Fitba' Loon's interest began to wane and one day, when the Bothy Loon, still full of enthusiasm, asked him "What do you think we should plant in that space over there?" he replied "I think we should put it into set-aside."

Now, the man who's really kept our garden blooming lovely over the years is Grandfather Bear. He's taking life a bit cannier these days, but he was 'a man for all seasons' who took a real pride in his work. When I first met him, he showed me round his garden and I was very impressed with the colour and freedom of his flower borders (I don't like things all sitting in regimented rows) and when I came to his beautiful bed of carnations I just had to pick one, for I love their spicy smell. Afterwards, in a light hearted gesture, I stuck it between Bramble the dog's teeth and she ran around grinning happily from ear to ear. I wasn't exactly grinning from ear to ear though, when I heard what happened later. Apparently, she'd kept going where I left off and the only bloom that was left standing was the one she had between her teeth. Luckily my future father-in-law saw the funny side of it all and our friendship flourished over the years. But, just remember – you can teach old dogs new tricks.

Probing Seeds Of Doubt

When I first thought about discussing Genetic Engineering in this article, my immediate reaction was. "Who? Me? Genetic Engineering? Come off it." However, the seeds of the matter had been sown in my mind and when Father Bear came in for his tea I said to him, You'll have to tell me all you know about Genetic Engineering." "Me?" he replied, "You're talkin' to the wrong man. The only engineering I know anything about is the kind you need spanners for." "But you must have read about it in all that farming bumph you get?" I insisted. "Not really, I tend to skip over it," was the reply. "Do you know anything about DNA then?" I asked. "Oh, I know plenty about them, that's where I get bits for the car." I could see I was flogging a dead horse.

After tea I sat down with a heap of farming magazines and leafed through them. (My, but they made depressing reading). Eventually, I found one or two snippets of information, but I realised that I'd need more, so, first thing next morning I saddled my horse and rode into town. Now, in the first 'country' office I went to, I could see the girl looking at me as if I'd crank written on my forehead when I asked for material on Genetic engineering. No, sorry, she didn't have anything at the moment, but she had the name and address of a man who did. Right, I thought, so far no good, I'll go to the library. The librarian whom I've know for some years was very helpful, and after spending an enjoyable ten minutes discussing the joys of country living I came away with the following two books. 'The Language of Genes' and 'The Genetic Revolution' (Today's dream or tomorrow's nightmare).

Now, I've never been one of your scientific types (apart from the amazing 95% I had for third year botany in the rock 'n' roll years) and the only thing I've examined recently is a mouldy bean struggling for life in a jam jar of cotton wool in an infant classroom. I thought I'd give what's left of the old brain cells a bit of a challenge, but after skimming through page after page of information, my head was reeling with reprogrammed cows, low fat pigs, self fertilising cereals, instant forests, viruses wiping out civilisation, and fish with mouse genes. (Now for my Genetically Engineered joke........ Which fish played 'The Yellow Submarine'?....The one with the moose organ, of course). My poor eyes felt as if they'd just knitted a kilt, but the gist of the contents were that man is trying to alter and improve all forms of life, without really knowing what the consequences might be.

Apparently, (that sounds quite good doesn't it) the earliest techniques of Genetic Engineering go back a long way, and animals have been cross bred for centuries. But, it was a curious Austrian monk called Gregor Mendel who, when pottering away among his monastery plants around 1860, decided to do a bit of pollen swapping and see what happened. After a time he found the new plants he'd created seemed to have hung on to the strongest features of their species, and only under certain circumstances was there any sign of the weaker ones.

When I was reading that, I suddenly realised that I'd been first introduced to Genetic Engineering when I was about six by one of my uncles, when he told me the following story about a farm cat who'd lost one of her front legs in an accident. "Ye see," said uncle, "she was a wonderfu' mooser, an' so the fermer made her a wee widden leg. Well, when she had her nixt lot o' kittens, each ane had a wee widden front leg, and ye should've seen thae little nippers when they were huntin'. They jist grabbit their prey wi' ae' paw, and then bashed it o'er the heid wi the ither ane."

Now that wee story seems harmless enough, but what about one of the true stories where a new gene has been added to 90 new varieties of potatoes to produce a poison which is lethal to the Colorado Beetle? It might not only be the beetles that have had their chips. Of course we all want what's biggest and best and healthiest for ourselves and our families, but I think we're engineering our own destruction.

Anyway, would two pairs of hands have made any difference to my life? I doubt it. Father Bear's been under the impression for years that I already have.

* * *

Please Don't Phone Again

Do you suffer from a never ending stream of phone calls like we do, from folk wanting to sell you a new kitchen or double glazing? Now, I don't know how many firms are involved in this telephone selling business, but you'd think they'd keep some kind of record or other so that they didn't keep phoning the same numbers again and again, wouldn't you? I mean, if I didn't want a kitchen yesterday, am I likely to want one next week? And, more to the point, how many kitchens do the average family need in one house anyway? I know it's a very true saying that two women should never share the same sink, but the only other female in our house is Buffy the cat, and her sole interest in the sink is the cupboard underneath it, because that's where I keep her food.

It's just the same with double glazing. If we've told our unseen callers once that we already have double glazing we must have told them a thousand times. I know we live in a windy place, but again, how many 'windies' can we cope with?

More recently, a new approach has been used (but we know fine it's just cauld kail heated up again). "If you were given the chance, free of charge, to replace your kitchen or windies (or something along these lines) which kind would you choose?" "Well, for the kitchen we'd like an old kitchen range that blows black reek when the wind is from the north, a big stone sink, two big presses and a table that seats a dozen. For the windies, we'd prefer to have glass, and thick wooden shutters." But, of course, at the end of the day I'd be about as well telling the crows to stop picking out the grain.

One evening, about three weeks ago, the house was full of starving bears all sitting watching 'Neighbours' and waiting for me to dish up their tea, when the phone rang. There I was, a pot of tatties in one hand and a red hot grill pan of spitting sausages in the other, but, as I was right beside the phone, I laid down the sausages and answered it. "Could you tell me," said a man's voice, very civilly, "the phone numbers you use most often" .... We were obviously in line for one of those "if you blether away, you've less to pay" offers, but his sense of timing made me want to tell him exactly what he could do with his phone numbers, although, I must admit, I did see the comical side of the situation. The bears, whose ears were flapping, began baying for beef, and shouting, "tell whoever it is to get lost," so, I told him politely (yes to my credit, I did) to phone back later at a more convenient time, but I think I must have given out bad vibes because we haven't heard another chirp from him since.

I have to say that Grandfather Bear has a wonderfully direct, and very successful way of dealing with all unwanted callers, but he too has his problems, because his phone number is only one digit different from that of a local taxi firm.

When I look back though, there have always been callers selling things. In days gone by, they came round the farms, occasionally in a van, but more often on foot, trying to persuade the womenfolk to buy their wares. I can remember the heavily bearded peddlars with their colourful turbans, whose battered cases bulged with brightly coloured clothing, and whose pockets were full of 'lucky' beads. The travelling folk too would come in about, and one memorable old couple, who had visited us for many years, never went away without a tasty bite from mother. One of their visits coincided with our pig having been killed and mother gave them a piece of roast pork but apologised for it being a bit fatty. "Oh, dinna worry my dearie," said the old body. (She did all the talking, he stood quietly in the background - some things never change). "The only thing we'll be sayin's wrang wi' it is, that it's jist a peety there wisnae mair o' it."

Perhaps, then, that's what's wrong with these faceless, anonymous callers of today; there's no character to banter and barter with, there's no shabby case or basket laid down on your doorstep, there's no little blackened billy can needing some hot water and there's no room for the weary, not even in the stable.

* * *

Time To Head Off To The Highland Show

Once again we have entered the season of Martyrdom and self denial. Yes, it's make your mind up time for Father Bear. Will he or won't he go to The Highland Show? First of all, we have to go through the usual palaver of, "Ye ken, it's getting' tae be a gey dear day oot nooadays, and I've mair than enough tae be getting' on wie here at hame withoot trailin' awa' doon tae Edinburgh." (At this stage I tuck the fiddle under my chin and play a lament for the man who cannot bear to leave his native soil behind and go over the water).

By early evening and after much soul searching, Braveheart has reached his decision......."Ach, we may as well jist go."

Next morning the cat's sussed out why her dishes are in the old greenhouse and she's not happy. Of course, we have a cat flap for her, but it's still lying in the cupboard in its cardboard box.

"Will I make up some pieces and a flask?" I ask Father Bear who's looking very clean and almost holiday like. "Aye, but go easy on the mustard." (He reckons I've got shares in a mustard company).

When I eventually go out to the car with my bits and pieces, I'm greeted with the fail me never "What's been keepin' ye woman?" and I rise to the bait in my usual way.

I can't remember how old I was on my first visit to the Highland Show, but I know it was at Inverness, and a man lifted me up on his shoulders to see the Queen, (No, no, it wasn't Victoria, it was The Queen Mother wearing a pink hat) so I must have just been a wee shrimp. (It would take a forklift to get me up that height nowadays).

So, what do I get out of The Highland Show? Well, sometimes I've come away home feeling tired and fed up, with my mother's famous, "If you've seen one show, you've seen them all," ringing in my ears, but, in all fairness, I think that applied to the days when I was trekking around with little Bruins, who were doing all the things that only little Bruins can do successfully. You know what I mean.

"Mummy, Mummy, I'm needing the toilet." Now, my heart always sank at that one, because, the nearest toilet was usually about half a mile away, and when we arrived there, the queue was always about 50 deep, (By that time of course, Father Bear had shot the crow with his usual...... "I'll meet you at the grandstand at 4 o'clock") and once you'd maneuvered yourselves in and out of cubicles that were surely designed for the matchstick people in Lowry's paintings, it was balloon time, because you'd foolishly promised it would be.

Now, I reckon that these bloomin' balloons cause more grief among young children than all the rest of the show put together. There's aye a crowd o' bairns sobbin' their hearts out and pointing to their prized possession which alas, is now no more than a black spec in the sky. One year our futile chase ended up with Bruin Two standing on top of a tractor, with a walking stick (borrowed from a bemused passer by) in his outstretched hand, frantically trying to catch the little Bruin's runaways before they went off into orbit.

In recent years, however, the Bruins have made their own way round the show and instead of having to stand queueing for drippy ice-creams and hot dogs I tag along with Father Bear. However, the outcome of this Darby and Joan act is that I sort of merge into the walls of hospitality caravans and try to look intelligent, while the men put the mechanical world to rights. As I sit there sipping scalding tea and covering myself with biscuit crumbs, I feel like something that's fallen off a flittin'.

Eventually, a jovial Father Bear lays down his glass and asks, "Have you seen the craft tent yet?" "No," I reply," I've been too busy counting the flowers on my skirt." "Right then, let's go and have a quick look round, before we go home." A quick look round-that's the understatement of the day. He flew past the dumplings and the four ply socks like a bat out of hell, and as we trudged slowly back to the car, he turned to me and uttered these three magic little words "Will you drive?"

* * *

Landscape Through A Holiday Makers Eyes

I'm sitting here relaxing in an old walled garden, set amongst fields of flowers, whose sweet perfume drifts gently towards me on the warm summer breeze. Little birds twitter happily in the hot, blue sky and from time to time, a heavily laden bee drones slowly by. Shimmering through the heat haze, the distant old medieval market town basks on the terraced hillside and away beyond its fruit groved horizon lies the sea.

By now, you're probably thinking that I'm sitting sunning myself in the Loire Valley or some such place, but sadly, no such luck. I'm just trying to make fields of oilseed rape and berry dreels sound exciting, for Father Bear is not a holiday person. The snag is, you see, he took his engineering skills to the merchant navy for a few years when he was footloose and fancy free and nowadays he reckons that folk are far better at home than "maybe going away getting bombed or shot or something!"

Having said that though, we have been on quite a few holidays, which you could say were memorable for all the wrong reasons.

On our first holiday, (when the two young Bruins were around nine and ten) we went to Tenerife in January, which seemed a great idea, but when we were there it snowed here, the real deep, solid, eighteen inches stuff, and he fretted all the time in case the weight of it would make the roofs of his broiler sheds cave in. We also hired a car – a little foreign affair, so that we could go sight seeing and one afternoon we were biffed in the rear end by a big, heavy, patrol truck thing, driven by a local of similar build. Well, Father Bear and the other driver jumped out of their respective vehicles and started shouting and waving and swearing at each other........Now, we don't speak Spanish, but, it wasn't hard to translate the gist of it however, to cut a long story short, the guy had been trying it on, because our little matchbox had hardly a mark on it, and his was dented and twisted, so the car hire company gave him his marching orders. (Also in Spanish.)

Our next holiday, a few years later, was to Jersey and we took Grandfather Bear with us. Now, I liked Jersey, (which was desperate for rain) but I'd have been better taking the cat than the four menfolk. They weren't into shopping; well, that came as no surprise. (They'll stand for hours at a roup, of course)! They weren't into beaches (sand jist gets in tae a' thing) and the highlight of the visit to the German Hospital was a Scottish car park attendant who waved "Jock's" hired car into one of the few parking spaces left. By the end of the week we'd only clocked up 84 miles as we criss-crossed the island like a crowd of sheep looking for fresh grass, and were on nodding terms with a windmill which we must have passed about a hundred times.

There was certainly no shortage of rain when the five of us went to Skye for our next holiday and that was probably just as well because Bessie, our faithful old car, began to cough and splutter with serious bronchial problems and had to be given great doses of water every few miles. Father and Grandfather Bear looked like a couple of two year olds who'd binged on a bag of liquorice as they regularly tried to blow the oily gunge from her tubes and reduce her temperature and funnily enough, we never saw one midgie.... they probably thought we'd had enough irritations for one week.

In Majorca, spectacular thunder storms ripped the sky apart, (the first rain for almost six months) and when we stopped to peep through a magnificent wrought iron gate on a country cycle run, we came face to face with the largest, meanest looking dog you've ever seen. He was obviously a big noise in the neighbourhood watch and before we'd time to get on our bikes, the whole place had gone barking mad.

Our three day trip to York impressed Father Bear, but the Yorvik centre didn't. "Fancy having to pay for a stink like that." (There have been worse stinks here many's a time, and no word about it!)

And where are we heading this year? Well, Father Bear is in the throes of excavating a site for a chicken shed, so it looks to me as if we'll just have to settle for the Costa Del Soil again.

* * *

As Wedding Day Approaches

"A'body likes a waddin,' a'body loves a 'do',
Ma granny does the eightsome reel, an ma granda' he gets fu'."

This little song keeps running through my mind these days as we finalise the preparations for Bruin One's 'waddin,' which is now less than a couple of weeks away. The new high heels are getting broken in, Father Bear and the Fitba' Loon are having another redd up and kindly folk arrive with beautifully wrapped parcels and boxes.

When I was young (and ate plain bread crusts to make my hair curl) mother's wedding gift to the happy couple was usually "A lovely square faced Westminster chimes clock," which went crazy every fifteen minutes and totally berserk on the hour, and I often wondered if the poor souls ended up stuffing it away in a cupboard or something before its eternal ding donging drove them daft.

In these same days gone by the local newspapers did wedding write ups which described, in some detail, what the bridal party had worn. My mother's all time favourite was when "The bride's mother (a very large lady) wore a two piece suit made of elephant crepe."

Because I was the youngest of about a hundred cousins and an only child, I was always invited to weddings and I can still remember my first outfit. I wore a plain pink velvet dress, a red rose and red shoes and I felt grossly over dressed because I normally ran around in old dungarees, a jumper and brown sandles. I can't remember much about the wedding, but the bouquets were so large that the bride and her bridesmaid resembled a couple of horses looking over a hedge.

My next wedding was a February 'do' and the outfit was a rusty brown tweed coat with a government health warning, and a kilt (bought in Perth's grandest store at sale time). The bride had the most beautiful bunch of pink tulips I'd ever seen and for weeks after that she was the subject of all my drawings, which I thought were real works of art with their curly hair and splayed feet.

When I was eleven, I was asked to be flower girl at a cousin's September wedding. Pleased just wasn't the word; I felt like a cow who'd landed in a bed of lettuce and I spent the whole summer dreaming of the big day. When it duly arrived, I fair thought I was the bees knees in my long, pale blue dress, my home perm and my single string of pearls (a present from the bride, although, to tell the truth, I much preferred the tank with two goldfish which the bridegroom gave me). But, and this really took the biscuit, instead of the huge, trailing bouquet I'd been expecting, I was handed a dainty little posy of anemones which barely covered my big hands.

Well the weddings and the years rolled by, and I saw it all. Some men were raged at for having a dram too many, others were in the dog house for removing their false teeth (which were fair gie'n them gyp) at the meal and a few completely disgraced themselves by "no gie'n 'The Wife' a dance."

The ladies always eyed up each other's finery and talked knowingly about "mutton dressed as lamb" and "black sheep." But I didn't know what they were on about, for we usually had steak pie and "Baa Baa" was the only black sheep I knew anything about.

A warm July wind rippled through the golden barley fields on the afternoon that Father Bear promised to share all this wordly goods, and we had a lovely time. But the icing on the cake came later, with my new Mother-in-law's tale of the suitcase. Apparently, some of the guests had sneaked into our changing room and stuffed the contents of 'my' case with confetti. Only, it wasn't my case, it was Mother-in-law's (who hadn't wanted her new outfit to get crushed on the journey) and she was just about doubled up with laughter at the impression 'my rather staid trousseau' must have created.

Last year, when the Ythan banks were yellow with broom, Bruin Two married his Bonnie Lass O' Fyvie, at "The best wedding ever." The sun shone, the champagne flowed freely, the fatted calf, which was roasted in a converted dung spreader, melted in the mouth and the guests danced the night away to "a real cracker of a band."

Well, it's time I stopped twittering on about the past and concentrated on the present. My 'Tartan army' can't see what all the fuss is about, and come the day of the 'match' they will sail forth without a care in the world and wonder why I can't do the same.

* * *

Born To Shop – But For The "Bear Necessities"

When I saw a car with a "BORN TO SHOP" sticker in its back window, I thought, that's me. However, once I'd had a look at the make of car and its glossy owner, I thought, no, that's not me. My "Born to shop" revolves round buying the 'bear necessities' for a crowd of guys who are no more into designer labels and nouvelle cuisine than the cat is into baking girdle scones.

I was eight the first time mother sent me for 'the messages' and as I free wheeled down to the village on my little Miss Jean Brodie bike, I felt like a dog with two tails (I did a lot of stupid things when I was eight, like learning to bake and milk the cow). Well, from then on, I became the local packhorse and the situation worsened when I went to Secondary School in the nearby town, because mother asked me to bring all sorts of weird and wonderful things. I don't think she realised what it was like to go into a butcher's shop and ask for pig's trotters and ox tongue and such like, surrounded by teenage girls who stood screwing up their faces as the offending articles were wrapped up in brown paper. And it didn't end there, because when we climbed on to the school bus the news quickly leaked out about the contents of my soggy parcel and I could have crawled under the seats. But, everyone has their ten minutes of glory and mine came, rather unexpectedly, the day I trauchled up the bus steps with a cheeping cardboard box containing 24 very lively day old chicks.

In these distant days before Andy Pandy, Looby Loo and Teddy climbed out of their baskets on to the television screen, mother also bought messages from a grocer's van which came round on a Wednesday and a baker's which arrived on Tuesdays and Fridays. Now I loved a Wednesday because that was when I got my 'School Friend' (a comic full of secret societies and lovable duffers) and two packets of plain crisps. But that was also the day that mother would scrutinise her message line to see if it had been added up correctly, and if she'd been overcharged by as much as one half penny, then I had, to my acute embarrassment, to run out with the offending bit of paper and stop the grocer on his return journey.

Father was a law unto himself when he was sent for messages and he never seemed to get a row. One summer day (when eskimos were the only folk with fridges) he was asked to bring a pound of fish, and he arrived back with four pounds. Another time he was told to bring back a bit of cheese, and he returned with a whole, big gouda, which was like leather before we'd reached the end of it. But his best ever mad buy was 28 pounds of cox's pippin apples which lasted for weeks and when their sturdy wooden box was empty I used it to make my first cairtie – a master piece of engineering – whose four iron wheels (pinched from a sheep hake) could be heard clanking down the bumpy road as it picked up speed.

Now, in those long-gone days of shimmering summers and wild winters, the shops had a wonderful smell. Everything sat on shelves waiting to be weighed or cut up, and the only forms of packaging were brown paper bags and string. Today, packaging is big business and we all want eggs from wee country cottages and butter from that happy herd of cows who could really make their marque in the field of line dancing.

Alas, Father Bear has never been into shopping and as I trundle my trolley up and down the Supermarket dreels I feel quite miffed when I pass a couple where the men actually say things to their wives like "Ah think we're needin' mair teabags" or "will I get anither packet o' yon nice biscuits we had last week."

However, one day, several years ago (when I still worked and didn't fiddle about all day) my elderly vacuum cleaner packed up in a cloud of stoor. I asked if he could go and buy me another one, and I over ruled his protest by announcing "No vacuum cleaner, no tea." "An what," he pleaded, "will I bring if they dinnae have that kind?" "Six pies" I replied. The new machine was there when I arrived home!

* * *

Only One Thing Forgotten

Well, the wedding's over, the glad rags that looked like a cross between Dallas and Dynasty are back in the wardrobe, the little boxes of cake have reached their destinations, the honeymooners are home and another harvest has begun.

And was our big day a memorable occasion? It certainly was and so was the day before, because, back in January, when we first began to plan the wedding, all the hotels were already booked and we decided to go for a D.I.Y. reception in the local hall.

Anyway, the day before the wedding dawned warm and sunny and there was a buzz of excitement about the house as we all set about our allotted tasks. The wedding flowers (including Grandfather Bear's best roses) were all looking very perky in their assorted tins and buckets, and the bridegroom's folks (who had very generously agreed to decorate the church and the hall) were due at any moment with another car load of blooms.

As everyone else was busy, I had to collect the hired kilts on my way to pick up the Bride and Groom to be, who'd been parking their car at the hotel where they were going to spend their wedding night.

Now, Father Bear had been very casual about these kilts. "Jist phone up an' get the same lot again." "But," I said, "Don't you want to try them on?" "Try them on! Whit on earth would we need tae dae that for. We're jist the same size as we were last time." Honestly, it was just like phoning in an order for tractor diesel. "Aye we'll have 600 gallons o' tractor diesel. Oh aye, an' anither thing, ye'll maybe throw in yon kilt ootfits we had the last time."

When we arrived back home there were phone messages to say that Bruin Two and his wife and Little Baby Bear were on their way, and Bruin Three and his two big cases would need picked up at the bus stop. Dinner was a quick chase round the kitchen before we raced off to the hall to unload the catering equipment van and prepare the tables.

After the bride had checked everything down to the last teaspoon, the friendly hall keeper and an ever growing band of helpers soon had the place looking fit enough for the Queen. The arrival of the two hard working flower folk and their very striking handiwork was the icing on the cake and because these willing souls couldn't stay for tea, we waved them off with a "cairry oot" of boiled tatties and steak pie.

Our next stop was a rehearsal at the kirk, where Father Bear observed (in no uncertain terms) that he would need to go for two new back tyres, first thing in the morning.

The rest of the evening passed in a happy mixture of family banter, cups of tea and clutter. Our one and only bathroom went like a fair as eight folk fought for their share of hot water and I found Buffy (the cat with the longest cleeks in the country) sitting on the end of the bridal veil with a mean smirk on her face.

Saturday's dawning was disappointingly dull, but at least it was dry. The bathroom braced itself for another stampede. Buffy was sick on the couch and poor Baby Bear was teething. An apologetic family whose car had broken down came to use the phone, the buttonholes and bouquets arrived, a present was handed in and (true to form) a double glazing salesman rang.

As we drove to the little country church I felt like I was in a dream, but when I walked between the pews of smiling guests I knew this was no dream. This was it. This was the wedding. The bridegroom's mother and I sat sharing a hanky as we watched the obvious happiness of our son and daughter, and when we slowly followed the handsome couple out of the church, the bothy loon announced, to my disbelief, that "Grandfather Bear was wearing a kilt."

The champagne was flowing when we arrived at the reception to welcome our guests, and a beautiful buffet meal awaited us. By the time the band arrived I could feel all the tension and worry of the past month beginning to drain away. Folk seemed to be enjoying themselves; they were chatting, they were laughing and they were dancing. Dancing! Oh. No. Suddenly it hit me. I'd come away without the money to pay the band. Ach well, maybe one of these days I'll be perfect.

Calm Little Corner In A Troubled World

"An' foo's yer bonnie flooers an' things daein' this year?" "Ach, they've been fair murdered wi' this awfy wither." I overheard this disheartening little conversation the other day between two couthy old lads who were standing next to me at the supermarket checkout and although I knew he wasn't struggling to make a living from his little crop, I still felt sorry for the old fellow who had seen the fruits of his labours and his chances of being a prizewinner at the flower show, dashed to the ground.

When I was little I can remember seeing old men just like him lovingly tending their 'dallies' and sweetpeas, and one hardy soul once biked all the way up to the farm for a wee bag of sheep droppings for his 'tamaties.'

Now, in a world as small as mine, a visit to the village flower show was quite an occassion and I was awful excited when the Mother Hen entered my name for some of the junior competitions. On the 'big day' it came as no surprise that I'd been awarded first prize for my hand knitted, sky blue socks because, although I say it myself, they were quite the finest you've ever seen. In fact, when the visiting needlework inspectress said she'd never seen such a well turned heel from a girl of my age, my face lit up like a beacon. Thankfully, and much to my relief, it never occurred to her that my roasting cheeks were caused by guilt and not pride, because, you see, I hadn't knitted the bloomin' things. My auntie (who lived with us) had. Now, Auntie was really nifty on the needles and when she saw the complete pig's ear I was making of things, she stepped in and saved the day, but warned me not to tell anyone. (However, she was real pleased on hearing that her work had been so much admired).

I fair thought I was the bees knees, though, when I saw that I'd won first prize in the handwriting competition. Mind you, that wasn't difficult, because, nobody else had entered it. And no wonder. For back in the good old days of dip, drip and scratch pens, writing out the Lord's Prayer wasn't for the faint hearted. I reached the Amen on my eighth attempt and by that time, the table was littered with rejected sheets covered in blots and mistakes. My hands and face were smeared with ink, I was nearly cross eyed, and I'd broken one of the Ten Commandments more than once.

When I moved round to the flower section more prizes awaited me, for I was first equal (out of two) for my wild flower collection and my model garden. By this time, as well as feeling important, I'd grown quite rich, too, because I'd made £1 in prize money.

As I was collecting my stuff one or two other folk who were also clearing up gave me some of their winning produce to take home, and this caused me a few headaches because I only had my bike. My handlebars were dangling with string bags full of 'ingins' and cabbages and 'tamaties' and things and to relieve my trauchle, I flung my model garden (which was balanced precariously across my front basket) unceremoniously into the first ditch I came to.

Oddly enough I've never put anything into a flower show since then, although I nearly did the year I had a magnificent, dark red and green velvety coleus. My showpiece sat in all its splendour on a south facing sill until the day that big Angus the cat decided to reverse in through the top of the open window. We'll, the stupid beast skited, and all eighteen pounds of him crash landed into the unfortunate plant. He didn't wait for the explosion!

I had a quiet, nostalgic wander round the local flower show at the weekend and in that calm little corner of such a troubled world, time almost seemed to have stood still. I could have been ten again and the realistc wee man made out of fruit and vegetables with his twinkling blackcurrant eyes could well have been mine. And when I reached the prize winning cloutie dumplings I almost duffed things up by breaking another of the Ten Commandments. Would anyone have pressed charges? And what would they have been? Maybe 'Loitering within tent' or possibly, Loitering with intent'? Well, there's always next year, isn't there?

* * *

The Days Of Rabbit Pie For Supper

"Jist come and see this!" I knew by the tone of Father Bear's voice the other morning that he'd found something quite unbelievable in the paper. "Jist take a look at that!" he said, stabbing his finger at the headline....."£1000 To Fund Rabbit Study." "Did you ever hear the like. The Cooncil's agreed tae contribute £1000 towards a project tae figure oot the best way tae eradicate rabbits." The Fitba' Loon, who'd been sitting waiting patiently for the two back pages joined in with his colourful tuppenceworth and I pictured millions of protesting rabbits hopping along the motorway with placards and banners. Rabbits have been part of my life for as long as I can remember and we had a sort of cottage industry going with them for many years. Father and I used to set snares on the hill, and on a windy night he would sit in his old arm chair and say. "Aye, they'll be runnin' weel the nicht." He was usually right too. But you know, rabbits are heavy and by the time we'd humped them all back to the farm we were like a couple of half shut knives. A big van came twice a week to collect them and by the time it left us it was usually stappit fu'.

During busy spells on the farm father sometimes asked the local rabbit trapper to help out, but the old lad was a bit like the Ancient Mariner, in that when he found a 'victim' he would think nothing of spending two or three hours spinning fantastic yarns of days gone by. However things improved greatly after he acquired a new dog, because, when it got fed up waiting for him it tugged the sleeve of his jacket. "Aye," commented my uncle, (a kindly man whose patience had been sorely tried over the years), "He's been far ower lang in getting that dug."

In the days before the humble rabbit had reached the sophisticated world of haute cuisine, and bairns ate what was put in front of them, it was part of our staple diet. I always thought mother's tasted better than anyone else's, because, after she'd cooked it she dipped the pieces in flour and fried them in a huge pan. However, after she saw poor, hunched up, bulging eyed rabbits sitting dying with myxomatosis at the road side she said she'd never eat another one.

I felt sorry for them as well, and although I was under no illusions about how destructive they were, I was still young enough to picture a cute little family of them sitting round their rustic table eating carrot cake and drinking dandelion wine.

They always won too, didn't they? When did you ever read a story about a rabbit who ended up a loser? Mind you, that's probably because most of them had I.Q.'s of at least 150. Fairy story land is littered with their victims, and every time I hear of a Mr. MacGregor I still think of Peter Rabbit.

Years ago when I worked at the chalk face, I read the famous Beatrix Potter story to a little boy whose speech was very limited and afterwards I asked if he could tell me what had happened. "Rabbit.....gairden.....no weel.....seek.....got row.....in bed." I gave him a gold star.

Now big Angus the cat was a great rabbit catcher when he was in his prime and one warm summer's day when all the doors were open, a rabbit came tearing into the kitchen with the big fella haring after it. This spectacular Tom and Jerry chase continued through the living room, out the front door, along the garden path and up the farm road. And then everything ground to a halt. For who should be standing there with his mouth open in anticipation but our neighbours' collie. Angus, the cat with attitude, simply flicked his tail, walked slowly back to the garden and lay down in the sun.

Around about that time Father Bear shot a rabbit with his rifle, and although it didn't escape, the bullet did. It whined right through the rabbit, ricocheted off a big stone and embedded itself in the radiator of our hard working little Dexta tractor, which immediately burst into tears.

Anyway, I'll be interested to hear the outcome of this forthcoming rabbit study. Will ferrets and snares and Grandfather Bear on his wee Fergie with attachments be a thing of the past? Will computerised warrens mean farmers can surf the net and delete their unwelcome tenants with a flick of their finger? I'll let you know.

Best Laid Plans "Gang Agley" Once Again

Three weeks ago, when I was preparing for our local festival, I warned my lot that they would just have to fend for themselves over the coming weekend because I wouldn't have time to run around after them.

You see, the problem is that this annual 'bash,' (which owes its origins to the Scottish folk music revival of the 1960s) always runs into harvest time, and as Father Bear and the two younger Bruins do a bit of outside contracting, my best laid plans don't just "gang aft agley" they usually end up going totally out of the window.

However, on Friday, it was too damp to combine or bale, so after Father Bear had coaxed the swather out of the foul mood it had been in all morning, he went off to cut two fields of oil seed rape.

Once the tea was over, I began to think, well, so far, so good. As soon as the Bothy Loon's ready we'll head up to the festival. Then the 'phone rang. It was Father Bear needing one of the Bruins to come along with the little red wagon and escort him to another field. So, as the Bothy Loon's singing could be heard above the roar of foaming bath water, I passed the message on to the Fitba Loon, who said in a flat kind of voice, "I was half thinking of going up to the festival too." I sighed. The familiar pattern was already beginning to emerge, and it was only 6.00p.m.

"Oh well, I suppose we could wait for you then," I replied, already resigned to the inevitable. (After all, what's half an hour out of a whole weekend?) "But for goodness sake don't be long, and take Father Bear's tea with you."

An hour later I went to look for him and in the distance I could see his little red wagon crawling along an old rutted track towards the main road, followed by a gey dour looking swather.

"It wasn't my fault," he peched, as he flung his clean clothes on with a graipe. "You see" . . . . . "Oh never mind" I replied exasperatedly, "just spare us the details and get a move on, I'm nearly two hours late."

The opening concert in the town hall was in full swing by the time we arrived and I made the usual string of apologies to my fellow committee members. Nobody bothered. They'd just assumed I'd be trekking round the countryside (like a harvest version of Santa Claus) delivering drums of diesel, net wrap, fish suppers and fags.

Anyway, after a wee while in the happy atmosphere I began to relax and enjoy the music and the company of those around me. However, by 2.00a.m. I just knew I'd have to call it a day and the two Bruins didn't protest much either at being dragged away from a fine singing and story telling session. But when we arrived home and saw what Father Bear had written on our notice board . . . . . "Lorry coming for grain at 6.45a.m." . . . . . we knew that Sod's Law had struck again.

Saturday morning dawned fair and fine and far too early, with the arrival of the grain lorry. I scuttered round making pieces and being driven slowly daft. The Bothy Loon who was keen to go to the festival declared that "A wee showrie or two o' rain around denner time wouldnae come amiss" and for once, the Fitba Loon, who was desperate to attend a league match, agreed with him.

Well, despite the warm sunshine, it was was still too damp for combining or baling and so, the Bruins (even without their "wee showerie o' rain") got lowsed for the day. And me......I was working on my next apology.

All afternoon the sun beamed down on the happy crowds who'd gathered in the square to listen to the instumental band. Informal groups of musicians played cheerfully for dancers and passers by. Competition prize winners were all smiles and the committee sighed with relief.

I was fair enjoying my high tea when a smiling Fitba' Loon appeared. "I've brought back the car, but I need a lift to Paul's house, an' can we go home first because I've forgotten to feed Buffy? Dinnae hurry yersel though, I'll see ye in five minutes."

Father Bear was at home and he'd fed Buffy, but he fancied chicken curry and fried rice. "Efter ye drop the Fitba Loon aff ye could mebbey...........Oh, an' if ye'll jist haud on till I get a bath and get shifted I'll come up tae the festival tae." When I returned he was fast asleep.

I could feel another apology coming on.

* * *

Gloom, Doom And Just One Thing After Another

It's a real damp, mizzley morning. I've been up since 4.30 a.m. and it's just a perfect day for havin' a real good goin' gloom, doom and misery session. And after all, why shouldn't I? Why should I go around with a smile that would put a horse to shame when other folk look as if they'd found a dead rat in their piece box?

Now, mentioning pieces to me at the moment is like waving a red rag at a bull, in fact it's probably worse. D'ye know, I've made thousands of pieces during this never ending harvest and now we're on to the tattie liftin' I think I'll write a text book on 'Problem solving' (the ' in thing' for school children at the moment) with examples like: "If a farmer's wife has a husband and two sons, and she makes up six slices of bread, three chocolate biscuits and a packet of crisps for each of them, every day of the week for ten weeks, how many loaves of bread will she use?"

But, it doesn't end at pieces, does it? Oh, no. They need drinks as well. Every day I ask them to bring back their empties, but what do I get? An armful when they remember and by that time the bottles look as if they'd been through the combine. So then I have to stand in front of a sink full of warm water submerging all these sticky, bashed, corked bottles until they pop back into shape again.

And talking about warm water brings me to another cross I have to bear. Washing working clothes. It really makes me sick when I see all these women on television saying they just can't believe their clothes are so white. I know why their clothes are so white. They were never bloomin' dirty in the first place. "Ground in dirt?" My lot are always lying on the ground in dirt. In fact, at this time of year they're a cross between clay cats, grease monkeys and Worzel Gummidge. And what about the guy who only needs to give his bath one wee squish of that wonderful cleaning stuff? If he'd to try, and scrape the oil slick off our bath he wouldn't be prancin' around looking so pleased with himself.

By now you'll probably think I'm getting steamed up about nothing but, you know, "it's jest been one darned thing after another." During these few, beautiful days of our Indian summer, a cowboy and two of his hands moseyed up from the south and dug up the part of our farm close which runs past the back door and the kitchen window, so that the electric cables and water pipes for our new chicken shed could be laid underground. Well, there I was, sitting like an Indian squaw, (not Minnie Ha Ha) beside all my water pots, gazing out over 'The Grand Canyon' while Big Chief Swathing Bear shot the crow. And, then, three days later, did my entire lifestyle not grind to a complete standstill yet again when he casually announced, before he disappeared. "Ye'll be mindin' that the electric'll be aff sometime this mornin." And when did it come on again? Half way through Coronation Street!

A couple of days later the car decided it wasn't well and began lurching around the close as if it was going to be sick. Father bear had various theories about cylinder headgaskets and women drivers, but in the end Jessie was hauled off to the garage where she stayed for three days to recover from some air flow burn out or other. I knew just exactly how she felt.

During her absence my choice of transport was shanks pony or the little red wagon, and everybody knows I've got to be desperate before I'll drive that thing. (I was desperate,) It's an awkward devil to steer, it's draughty, it's got all the junk of the day in it and it's never liked me since the day I said I wouldn't be seen dead in it.

A flying visit to Auld Reekie on Saturday night to see the Bruins and marvel at Little Baby Bear's abseiling skills, turned sour when I realised that I'd left Father Bear's mobile phone on their kitchen table. And when we got home Buffy the cat glowered at us from our unmade bed.

Well I suppose I'd better go and get on with some work. The vacuum cleaner bag's just about burstin'. The back door scraper's caked wi' gutters and the wally dugs can hardly see their feet for stoor. Life can be a real scunner at times.

* * *

Horror Tales Of Hallowe'ens Past Fail To Dim Mother's Enthusiasm

Hallowe'en

"I mind foo often we hae seen
Ten thoosand stars keek doon atween
The nakit branches, an' below
Baith Fairm an' bothies hae their show,
Alowe wi' lichts o' Hallowe'en".

"There's bairns wi' guizards at their tail
Clourin' the doors wi' runts o' kail
And fine ye'll hear the skreichs an' skirls
O'lassies wi' their drookit curls
Bobbin' for aipples i' the pail".

These two verses from Violet Jacob's wistful poem....Hallowe'en....conjure up wonderful pictures in my mind of my favourite time of year. I love the long, dark nights. The shivering starry skies. The clouds scudding silently across the moon's cold face and the smell of the land as it lies glistening under its blanket of frost.

Perhaps my love for all these things was kindled when, as a spellbound five year old I sat at my little ink stained wooden desk listening to the Mother hen weaving wonderful, spooky stories about evil witches soaring through the velvet night on their birken broomsticks and the wicked deeds of goblins and fairies who terrified country folk on All Hallow's Eve....that dreaded night before All Saints day.

Throughout my childhood years the school Hallowe'en party was one of the highlights on my sparse social calendar and I spent the week leading up to it making my fancy dress, which was usually a real "silk purse out of a sow's ear" affair. One year I made a witch's hat out of newspaper and then I painted it with this awful, black lacquer stuff I found in a little tin. What a smell it had! The whole place reeked for days and I must have been a real fire hazard as I skipped happily around the big classroom with my millinery masterpiece, my black rags and my jaggy broomstick. Another time I laboured so long over a Red Indian head-dress that the hens began to nudge each other in alarm when they saw me heading in their direction.

Of course, no outfit was complete without a neep lantern and for that, I was prepared to trudge up and down the dreels of swedes for hours, if need be, until I found the perfect specimen. Searching was the easy bit. By the time I'd finished hacking away at my neep, my thumb was just about falling off and my nostrils were filled with the smell of its creamy coloured flesh for the rest of the night. Mind you, that was tame to the singeing reek that arose when the grinning purple face began to cook.

My lantern making didn't end with my childhood either. Each year I made one for the Bruins, but, when I was looking at a box of fine, fat pumpkins in the supermarket the other day I just knew I'd been born too soon.

Out of my four Bruins, the Fitba Loon was the only one who shared my love of dressing up and I always accompanied him to the chalkface Hallowe'en party. One year I dressed up as a 'Punk' and I was a gey orra lookin ticket I can tell you, with my black makeup, weird hairdo, wayout clothes and ripped fishnets. Anyway, when we returned home that Friday night, Father Bear was waiting for a lift to the local hostelry and as I dropped him off I said in a peeved voice. "I notice you're not inviting me in tonight." "Ye'r jokin" he replied with a look of total horror on his face. "You wouldnae dare come in looking like that." "Wouldn't I?" I replied.

Well, I don't think I've ever seen Father Bear so mortified and what made it even worse for him was that, initially, nobody recognised me. There was a stunned silence as he pushed through the crowded lounge bar like a horse with blinkers on, not daring to look to right nor left, while I hobbled behind in my short, tight skirt. Folk looked on in total disbelief and then averted their eyes as he turned round with beads of sweat on his forehead and slapped a glass of orange juice in my hand.

Alas, my family have forgotten the magic of Hallowe'en and if they found me making a pumpkin lantern they'd probably think I'd gone doolally. However, each evening after dark, Buffy the cat and I have been tearing across the barley stubble trying to get 'Operation Thermals' off the ground. Nobody has twigged what we're up to, but let's just say that given a fair wind and a clear sky on Saturday night we could be heading your way.

An Alternative Solution To Looming Festive Pressures

There are only forty-six shopping days left until Christmas. Have I been counting them? No, I haven't, but I was unfortunate enough to bump into one of those scunners who told me that her presents are wrapped, her cards are ready to post, her freezer is full of Christmas baking and she's chosen her turkey. Well, I thought, uncharitably, I hope it runs away. I know, I know, that's a terrible way to think in this season of goodwill and everything, but that's just the point. It isn't the season of goodwill yet, is it? It's not even the middle of November.

Now, don't get me wrong, I've always loved Christmas and I don't think I fall into the Scrooge category, but nowadays many folk are worn away to a frazzle before it even arrives.

When I was little (and Tammy Troot ruled the air waves) our presents and cards were never bought until around the second week in December. When their big 'shop 'til you drop' day arrived, Mother and Auntie, and an assortment of bags and lists, would set sail for Perth with Father, who let them off at the top of the High Street on his way to the market. Mind you, the pair of them were always very relieved to get that length, for he was an awful driver and most of the time Mother had to "keep reminding him to keep his een on the road in front o' him and stop lookin' in a'body's fields." Some things never change, do they?

In those days most folk didn't have the money to lash out on expensive gifts but their simple offerings were chosen with care and given with love. (And yes, looking back on it, I suppose even those who give me boring hairy vests and dark grey knee length socks had my best interests at heart too).

So why in this age of Back to Basics, Going Green and Saving the Planet, can't we just Cut the Commercials and leave Christmas where it used to be?

Every magazine you pick up from October onwards is full of hints on how to have your best Christmas ever. The supermarkets have wall to wall biscuit tins and boxes of chocolates before Father Bear's even asked for his long drawers. Frantic parents are combing the stores so that wee Erchie, who can hardly find his bed among all his electronic gear in his room, will get this year's 'in toy'. And the fashion conscious are trying to lose a stone in weight so that they can get into 'That little black dress'. Little black dress! That's a laugh,- forget about the black, I haven't been able to get into a little dress since I was about nine year old.

I'll tell you who I feel sorry for nowadays....Santa Claus. In fact I reckon the poor old devil must be just about stressed out of his mind. He used to do a few parties here and there before the big delivery day, but just look at him now. He has to go around gaffering all these look-a-likes who sit in cardboard grottoes for six weeks before Christmas handing out presents and Ho-ho-hoing away to never ending queues of enthusiastic parents and fed up bairns.

But while I'm still on the subject of presents, did you know that in a recent newspaper survey, the two least popular were cheap perfume and aftershave, followed by, surprise surprise . . . . . handkerchiefs, bubblebath, ties and cardigans. Surely they didn't need a survey to reach that conclusion.

I've had enough bubblebath over the years to float the Q.E.2, and as for hankies....How is anyone supposed to blow their nose on these delicately embroidered bits of lace covered in wee pink rosebuds? You'd be about as well using one of these paper doilies that folk put cakes on. I'll not go into the aftershave, ties and cardigans situation, but just let's say I know a few men who could.

Now, here I am sitting laying off about Christmas preparations starting far too early when it's probably high time that I began thinking about what I'm going to buy for everyone. All I've got at the moment is a packet of ten cards with three right dour lookin' kings on them....but, I've just had a wonderful idea.

"It's still six weeks 'til Christmas time
I ken that by the date.
Forget yer scent and handkerchiefs
I'm off tae hibernate."

"An' when I'm in ma mossy nest
Ye neednae peety me
For I'll no need yer bubble bath
Nor turkey salad tea."

* * *

Bearing Up Under The Strain

"The mobile phone you are calling has been switched off. Please try again later." You know, that wifie's voice gets me fair fizzing. "Try again later." Oh aye, and a fat lot of good that polite suggestion is when there's an anxious lorry driver standing on the door step poring out some tale of woe or other and Father Bear is incommunicado.

And, of course, nine times out of ten (after I've either managed to sort things out or made a complete hash of them), he'll phone up with his usual chirpy enquiry. "You havnae been trying tae get me, have ye? Ma phone's been switched aff!" The other, and just as aggravating reply from the wifie is......... "It has not been possible to connect you." That, can mean anything from Father Bear hasn't heard the blasted thing, to it's lying in the little red wagon or left on top of the diesel tank in the shed.

Of course, the need to communicate has been with us since the world began and if we'd lived over two millenniums ago Father Bear would have come stoorin' round the corner of the close in his chariot (which is still in the grain shed) with the news that legions of men were roamin' about the countryside forcing folk to join 'The Commonus Marketus'. In later years he'd have been lighting a bonfire on top of the hill to pass on important news, or frantically trying to burn his fields before folk arrived to cause trouble. (He's still doing that). But, out of all the many and varied means of communication throughout the ages.............arrows, drums, flags, mirrors, morse, pigeons, gunfire, and so on, there is one which conjures up a wonderful picture in my mind. Him sending smoke signals.

Oh I can just picture the scene; Big Chief Swearing Bear and his wee, strippit, singed blanket fu' o' holes, coughing and spluttering on the top of some high ridge while the swirling wind blows his words back in his face. And would I know what he was trying to say? Of course I would. His messages haven't varied much over the years "Big Chief need tobacco for um pipe of peace....... .....Big Chief on warpath.........he tell squaw many times.......he no like um big heap green leaves on bread ....He only like buffalo on bread." See what I mean!

Now, it's all very well laughing and joking about communication but to tell you the truth, I'd be far happier sending a pigeon with a note tied to its leg than trying to master the art of the mobile 'phone. You see, I'm about as happy amongst modern technology as 'Catweazle" was (remember the television series about the mannie who was fair forfochen trying to cope with life in the 20th century) and matters are even worse since Father Bear bought a new, more sophisticated phone. I mean, can you tell me how I ended up with a wifie enquiring which emergency service I required, when all I had done was dial our own home number? The Fitba' Loon, who was in the car with me, couldn't figure it out either. I'm afraid in my case, new tricks are best left to young dogs. Just take the Bothy Loon for example. During the harvest we hired a mobile 'phone for him to use when he went off on his bailing exploits. And would you believe it, within half an hour of getting the blooming thing, he had figured out how to make it play everything from Captain Pugwash to The William Tell Overture and make tea. Makes you sick doesn't it?

However, Father Bear would soon tell you that it's a pity I don't have as big a problem with the spoken word as I have with the technology surrounding it! Words like 'hind legs' and 'donkeys' spring to mind, and he's still doubled up laughing about the phone call he had last Friday from Wee Baby Bear's Grandad up north. After the pair of them had sorted out the problems of the agricultural world, Grandad from up north asked if Father Bear knew when Wee Baby Bear and her parents were due to arrive 'in by'. "Oh, I'm no very sure on that" was the reply. "But, Mother Bear'll ken, I'll get her tae hae a wee word wie ye." "Oh heavens, dinnae dae that," pleaded the voice at the other end of the phone. "Can ye no jist ask her?" Men!

* * *

Thoughts Turn To Better Long Dark Nights

After I'd closed the curtains last Sunday night I settled down in my chair to have another look at the papers before I started making the tea. The living room was warm and cosy and Buffy was purring away on my knee when the Fitba Loon came rushing in at break-neck speed leaving all the doors open. "Dad says it's O.K. if I go to the match," he peched. "Could you run me in for the bus? It leaves at 5 o'clock." "And what about your tea," I enquired? "Och, dinnae worry aboot ma tea. Ah'll get something....somewhere," he shouted breathlessly, as he disappeared up to his bedroom to change into a United supporter.

An hour later a tired, weary and frozen Father Bear appeared. He flopped down on the sofa with a paper and fell fast asleep. I really felt quite guilty when I thought of him beavering away on his own out in the nearly finished chicken shed (which would make the Q.E. 2 look like a rowing boat) and so, after we'd eaten, I halfheartedly asked if he was needing a helping hand. He hummed and hawed about my offer but he must have decided it was better than nothing and said, "Aye, O.K. then, ye can scatter the water when I'm polishing the concrete." I don't get offers like that every day!

"Right," I replied, "I'll be out as soon as I've done the dishes." And after I struggled into two old coats, a pair of splattered wellies and a faded tammy that had seen better days, I set off to join him.

Now, I'm the one who always says she loves the long, dark, winter nights when the heavens are alive with stars, and the clouds go scudding across the moon. Of course, there was no moon that night, and although Orion and The Plough were sparkling like diamonds in the frosty air, they were precious little help to me as I shuffled slowly across the close towards the dark, looming shape of the shed. And that wasn't the worst bit of it. Oh no, I still had to cross the lunar landscape which surrounded it. Well, as I lunged into craters, splashed through the Sea of Tranquility and skited up the guttery moon mountains I began to feel a bit like yon three legged 'Jake The Peg' bloke that Rolf Harris used to sing about. By now, of course, I can guess what's going through your mind - why on earth did the silly ass not have a torch? Why did I not have a torch? Is there any need to tell you where all the torches were? I thought not.

Anyway, when I eventually arrived, Father Bear and his concrete polisher were flying around in circles like a bat out of hell, and above the deafening roar of the machine's clattering blades, he tried to shout and point to where he wanted the water sprinkled. Sprinkled! Believe me he's never been nearer getting a pailful of water flung over him in his life! However, after a couple of hours had dragged by (time fair flies when ye're enjoyin' yersel') a rather dejected Fitba Loon returned and Father Bear announced that I would drive the digger while they prepared the earthen floor for another hundred acres of concrete. And so, after I'd clambered up to my lofty perch, the Fitba Loon appeared at my elbow and gave me my first digger driving lesson.

"Right," he said pointing to things. "That's forrit. That's back. That's up. That's doon. That's swivel and that's it, O.K.?"

Now apart from forgetting to steer when I reversed and nearly knocking down the Fitba Loon when I went "forrit" I wasn't too bad, but by midnight my mind began to wander back to better, long dark nights than this.

Nights when mother and father and auntie and I would be sitting toasting our feet in front of a blazing beech log fire while we were listening to the wireless, or reading the papers or playing cards. Nights when mother had made smooth, creamy tablet and nights when a cosy hot water bottle warmed up my crisp, cotton sheets. Nights when...........................

"Back - Back - BACK - BACK - HOY - PEY ATTENTION. YE'RE NO SLEEPIN' ARE YE? WE'RE JIST ABOOT FEENISHED," shouted Father Bear.

"AND SO AM I," I yelled back. They were too busy shovelling sand out of the digger bucket to hear me. Ach well, it's not everyone that can say they've had a "big step up at the work" overnight.

* * *

Fond Memories Of The School Nativity Play

They came from far and near on that cold, winter's morn to gather round the humble stable where the baby lay. Mary, with a mother's instinct, wrapped the shawl lovingly round her little bundle and Joseph, who wasn't quite into the responsibilities of fatherhood was scanning the crowd to see if his granny had been able to get off her work.

There, in the pin dropping silence, everyone waited anxiously for the sign. ......The sparkling angels hovered on the wing........The shepherds tucked their lambs tighter under their arms......The animals nodded their heads and the three wise kings stood tall and regal in their brocade curtains.

"Right," whispered a kindly voice in my left ear. "We're ready. Take your time. Everything'll be fine. Remember .... just keep calm."

"Keep calm!" How on earth could I keep calm when there were about a thousand folk sitting out there watching and waiting for me to get the show on the road. My palms were sweating, my throat felt as dry as a basket and I'd lost count of the times I'd visited the wee room along the corridor. However, I knew that I had to face the music and so, after taking a deep breath, I stretched my trembling hands over the piano keys and began to play 'Silent Night'.

Now, I know fine that the loving relatives who come along to a school nativity play are not even remotedly interested in the prima donna at the pianna, in fact, I'm quite sure that one of the monkeys who advertise the tea could sit there and no one would give them a second glance.

Two or three years back, I was half way to Bethlehem with my "Little Donkey" and just beginning to relax, when the Headmistress came rushing across the hall shouting - "Stop! Stop playing the piano! We've to evacuate the building." My first thought was, surely my playing can't be that bad. Then I decided it must be a wind up, or maybe even 'Game for a Laugh'. It wasn't. One of the big heaters upstairs had gone on the blink. Strangely enough, my first encounter of the Nativity kind didn't come until the Fitba Loon was the oldest boy in the playgroup, and as such, was destined to play the part of Joseph. Well, the thrawn little devil dug the sandals in at this promise of early stardom and said "NO." So, after spending ages trying to persuade him, I eventually said "But, somebody's got to be Joseph." "Well," he replied very slowly, "it's no' gonnae be me anyway!"

Well, it came to pass (eventually) that it was, and as he sat there glowerin' at an equally reluctant Mary over a bale of straw, I never thought I'd see him in a dishtowel and strippit frock again. However, I was wrong and the following year the Bothy Loon and him were shepherds in the Sunday School Nativity Play. After their first rehearsal he came to me and said, "Do you know this, they're doing that same play again."

Talking about the way a child's mind works reminds me of a lovely wee story concerning a little chap who'd sat spellbound in class listening to the events of the first Christmas. When he returned to school after the holidays he went out to the teacher and in a voice full of concern enquired "His there been ony word o' yon fowk findin' a hoose yit?"

Many, many years ago, around Nativity time, Grandfather Bear had a wonderful find when he was dumping rubbish in the skip. He came across a fur coat. Well, he arrived all smiles and announced "I've got a braw coat fur ye the day. Jist tak a look at that. Ye'd wonder wha wid fling a thing like that oot, widn't ye?"

I nodded. It was built for the slim Twiggy lookalikes of the sixties with its shiny gold buttons, nippit waist and hood and one look told me that I'd have about as much chance of getting into it as the Ugly Sisters had with Cinderella's glass slipper, but rather than disappoint him I tried it on. "Aye, ah doot it's ower wee," he observed. "Wid it dae for onybody else?" Suddenly, I knew exactly who it would do for .... the donkey in the school nativity play.

A Merry Christmas and A Guid New Year tae ye a'.

Hit By The Flu Bug

When I was wee I was a right hardy little tyke, which was just as well, for Mothers in those days had precious little time to spend on ill bairns. Their recipe for good health was to feed a cold, starve a fever and dish out a pudding spoonful of Syrup of Figs every Sunday night (whether it was needed or not). The Fitba Loon chuckled with laughter when I told him the sad story of the regular Monday morning toilet queue at our little country school. The Bothy Loon quipped in with his favourite "Aye Mither, times were hard, but folk were happy" phrase and I'll better not tell you what Father Bear said.

Well, I certainly wasn't happy last Christmas Eve when I was knocked sideways by that nasty 'flu' which was going around. I still had a bit of last minute shopping to do including the two younger Bruins' presents and I'd planned to make a really special tea for Bruin Two and his wife (The Quinie) and Wee Baby Bear, who were spending the night with us before heading north on Christmas morning.

"We'll go an' get yer messages an' things if ye jist write doon what ye're needin'" offered the Bothy Loon. "Aye," replied the Fitba Loon....... "Ah'll drive if he gets the stuff." The pair of them set off in high spirits and returned in equally high spirits about an hour later. "We managed tae get everything ye wanted, but there was nae lettuce or greenery o' ony kind left so we just got a bag o' mixed peppers." Their hearts were in the right place.

By that time I was feeling so awful that I had to drag myself upstairs to bed. My head felt as if someone was hammering a fence post into it. My throat was raw and jaggy every time I swallowed. My bones were aching and I was sneezing and snottering in every direction, much to the annoyance of Buffy the cat who'd joined me for a bit of shut eye.

Later that evening Bruin Two said that when they arrived and saw Father

Bear slaving over the kitchen sink they thought I must have died!

I laughed in spite of my raspy throat and throbbing head, but his words took me back to the awful 'flu' I had when he and Bruin One were young. One night when I was at my lowest ebb, the strings of my old guitar which was lying flat in the corner of the dark bedroom, began to ping very gently. This is it, I thought, as I lay frozen to the spot. I'm passing over and there's not bloomin' soul here to say cheerio. I waited for the famous "your whole life will flash before you" bit. But it didn't. Something else did though........Florence the Hamster. The little beggar had escaped from her nightly assault course round the living room and headed fast for pastures new. While she was investigating the inside of the guitar she came across six little 'parallel bars' and had a wonderful time of it swinging from string to string like some spirited Saturday night Gladiator.

Now, although 'flu' was rife in schools during the winter time, I seldom took it and I remember the morning two very serious little Primary 1 girls came into my half empty classroom. One of them said "Pleath Mith, my brother Neil won't be at thcool today." "Oh dear," I said "has he got the 'flu'?" "Yeth," she replied. "He'th got the barkin' doggieth." I managed to keep a straight face.

Now, it's probably just as well that I don't take 'flu' often because the standard of nursing care in our house leaves a lot to be desired. I remember lying patiently waiting for a little appetising morsel for my tea one night, but when it finally arrived, it was a great, greasy, half cold fish supper and a slice of butter with a bit of torn bread hanging from it. The bread had obviously been hurriedly folded over and as I lay gazing at it in disgust it slowly began to open up.

"Ye surely havnae gone very far intae yer tea!" exclaimed Father Bear when he reappeared about an hour later. "Ye ken ye'll no get better if ye dinnae eat something. Ah'll no throw it oot, ye'll maybe fancy it at supper time."

Why did the words "Feed a cold and starve a fever" flash through my mind?

* * *

No Chickening Out Of This Special Opening

Well folks, today's the big day. At 2.30 this afternoon you can just picture me teetering across the close in my peerie heels, fur coat and tiara, to perform the official opening ceremony of my spanking new broiler chicken shed and giving the 34,000 new occupants their blessings. (The Queen said if she'd been on holiday at Balmoral instead of Sandringham she'd have come in by and Tony Blair's reason was that he was totally engulfed in other matters. So, I thought, I'll not be stuck, I'll just be like the Little Red Hen and "Do it myself."

Now, I know many of you will ooh and aah at the thought of all those fluffy little day old chicks scurrying across acres of warm wood shavings as they spread their wings in their new surroundings, but I'm afraid I'm not a big fan of anything with feathers on it. In fact, my dislike of hens and things of that ilk goes ' way back to the days when I was little enough to look them in their beady, unblinking wee eyes. They would stand and glower at me with that totally vacant stare of theirs and then, for no apparent reason, they'd give me a sharp peck on my thin, bare legs or go for my brown shoelaces. Every morning in life my mother flung tattie peelings out on to the dump and, before she'd even had time to scrape out the basin, this brainless posse of assorted 'gaun aboot' hens would come tearing across the close at breakneck speed only to find that it had been the usual time wasting exercise.

Anyway, to get back to the present. How am I feeling today? Will I maybe be filled with nostalgia when the big heated van full of fluffies rolls quietly into the close? Well, to be honest, I still can't believe that we're going back into broilers again. In fact, for years I've been saying that if any burds ever came about the place then this burd would be taking off!

You see, for the first thirteen years of our marriage, our life was overflowing with bloomin hens. (Broilers, layers, breeders, whatever, ...they were all hens to me). The big event on our social calendar was the poultry ball and although everyone got dressed up to the nines, you knew that the whole evening (apart from giving the "Birdie Dance" laldy) would be spent knee deep in hens' problems. And of course, it goes without saying, that the 'auld hens' sat soberly on their perch all night so that they could drive the big roosters home.

However (and this is probably where I'm losing my grip on reality), I am assured by Father Bear and the army of knowledgeable men involved in the construction and completion of my "Millhennium Dome" that hens don't have any problems any more. And even if they did, the wee T.V. screen (Channel Chix) in my living room would pin point any little hiccup that might arise. Isn't that a comforting thought? It'll be about as exciting as watching the proverbial paint dry.

It's a funny thing, but you know, before I married Father Bear I went to a fairground fortune teller wifie (the two events were totally unconnected) and she told me, among other things, that my hands were full of property. Now, as it turned out, all her short term predictions came true and that set me wondering about this property lark.

Property, to me, was a beautiful old sandstone mansion house, with velvety lawns and great spreading oaks sloping down to a lazy, meandering river. Property, was an elegantly curved terrace of pale, grey Georgian houses on the affluent side of the town, or better still, property was a beautiful white villa lying basking on a wooded, Mediterranean hillside. I could already see the impressive addresses embossed at the top of my vellum writing paper.

Now, I'm not going to dispute the wifie's mutterings about property, but gradually over the years the penny has dropped. My 'Property' is, and was always going to be ....a great assortment of bloomin' hen sheds.

Do you know that over the past twenty years I've seen thirteen hen sheds come and go, and the disasters and calamities and aggravations and swearings that I've lived through would have knocked the spots of any of your current soap opera ratings.

But, I'm a tough old bird and not one for chickening out of my responsibilities, and so, this afternoon you will see me, striding Boadicea like, up the slope towards the 'enemy' with a pair of shears in one hand and a bottle of cheep plonk in the other.

Too Many Visitors For The Kettle To Cope With

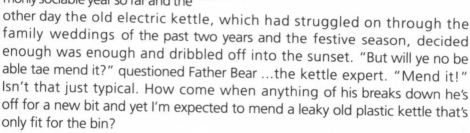

1999 has been an uncommonly sociable year so far and the other day the old electric kettle, which had struggled on through the family weddings of the past two years and the festive season, decided enough was enough and dribbled off into the sunset. "But will ye no be able tae mend it?" questioned Father Bear ...the kettle expert. "Mend it!" Isn't that just typical. How come when anything of his breaks down he's off for a new bit and yet I'm expected to mend a leaky old plastic kettle that's only fit for the bin?

Now, over the years we've spent many an enjoyable hour with folk who have dropped in to the kitchen for cuppies and a crack, but since the 34,000 little occupants of the Millhennium Dome arrived, everyone from the bairns down the road to the Bank Manager have come in by. I was just about ankle deep in stoor and woodshavings when the latter arrived at the back door, but when I asked him if I could afford a 'cleaning lady' he was a wee bit non commital.

I remembering suggesting to a previous Bank Manager who came to see us that we were in an ideal situation to establish a Country (Western) theme park. "Yee Ha." Well, that man just looked at me like I'd jumped up and Line Danced across the old dresser to 'The Tractors' beltin' out "Tulsa Time" and I could see that my Grand Ole Opry an' Nashville seeds were falling on the wrong side of the cotton pickin' track. But you know, I still think he was wrong, because, Clint Bear would have been very much at "Home on the Range." Bruin Two plays a mean moothie and blues guitar. The Bothy Loon (alias the "Rhinestone Ploughboy) would have been big on the bothy ballads of the Bayou and the Fitba Loon, well he'd have had the Hillbillies and the Honkey

Tonkers in a Five-a-side shootout before you'd time to tune a banjo. (Did you

ever hear the story about the dog who dropped into a saloon bar, placed a bandaged foot on the counter and said .... "Bartender....Ah've come to find the man who shot ma paw". I know, it's terrible, isn't it.?)

Now, I must tell you my two favourite stories concerning folk who've dropped in to see us, and although they happened many years ago I still cringe with embarrassment when I think about the first one.

Way back in the days before the younger Bruins were at school, the three of us had been in the town shopping and when we returned home I told them just to dump everything in the kitchen. Well, the place was in a right state with stuff lying everywhere, when I noticed a car with a couple of strangers in it drawing up at the garden gate. Oh no, I thought, I'll have to try and get rid of some of this junk, so I hurriedly gathered up the whole lot, flung it unceremoniously into the bathroom and shut the door.

Seconds later I was standing on the doorstep being introduced to a new feed rep and to my utter dismay, he turned to the elderly lady beside him and said ...."This is my mother, I brought her with me for a run and she'd wondered if she could maybe use your toilet?"

My other story took place one evening when a man, whom I'd never met before, called to see Father Bear. In our usual way we chatted away to him, but we began to realise that he never actually said anything other than "Aye." However, these "Ayes" managed to express all his answers wonderfully well even though the conversation was pretty lopsided and Father Bear and I began to sound a bit like a couple of excited budgies. He seemed in no hurry to go and it was a long time after supper when he finally took his leave. "Aye," he said, as he headed off into the darkness, "Thanks very much, ah've ha'en a braw nicht. Cheerio."

Well, all this talk about visitors and tea is making me feel fair hungry, so I'm away to plug in my beautiful shiny new kettle (yes, Father Bear's grudgingly admitted it's a good pourer) and have a big chunk of dumpling. Oh my goodness, there are two corgies coming across the close! It couldn't be..........could it?..............

* * *

Nothing To Wear Apart From Dusters

I was in the middle of washing the breakfast dishes the other morning when the Fitba' Loon came in and said, "We've tae go and tidy oot the 'milk hoose." "We," I snapped. "What d'ye mean 'we'? Do you think I've got nothing better to do than help you to clean out that pigsty of a place?" "Oh, it's no me that's botherin', like," he replied casually, "but Dad says you'll ken best whit's a' needin' tae be flung oot."

Well, that just made my day, for the milk hoose, which hadn't been cleaned out for years, was stuffed to the gunwales with an unbelievable assortment of stuff ranging from mildewed mattresses to tattie baskets full of burst footballs.

"And does it have to be cleaned out today?" I asked. "Aye," replied the loon, "thae rolls o' paper for pittin' the wee chickens' feed on is tae be stored in there." See these blinkin' birds, they've ruled the roost since the day they arrived.

Ten minutes later the Fitba Loon came bouncing round the corner with the loader and bucket to where I stood spitting feathers and looking tres chic in a coat which was fashionable when Ally McLeod took his Tartan Army to The Argentine.

"Dinnae pit thae oot," he shouted as I heaved a box of torn clothes into the 'skip'. "They'll dae fine for dusters." Dusters! I might have known dusters would come into it. You'd think that a crowd of men who are such staunch supporters of the 'Dusters Preservation Society' would have some respect for their own clothing, but not a bit of it. You'll find jumpers and jackets and boilersuits etc. etc. lying here, there and everywhere and they're all so filthy that they've begun to blend in with their surroundings. Then, of course the cry goes out that "we've run oot o' claes" and after I've read my usual riot act a tangled heap of greasy garments turns up anonymously on the back doorstep. (It's like something out of 'The Broons').

Now what really riles me about the whole business is that I've spent half my life trailing round shops buying working clothes for the three men and I've never had so much as an ounce of gratitude. They're that bloomin' fussy too,- you'd think they were going to a royal garden party or something, the critical way they examine everything.

Father Bear's bending and stretching antics when he's trying on a new boilersuit remind me of one of yon wee monkeys that jump up and down on bits of elastic, but, he has to go through this palaver before he decides if it's "A' richt" or "Ower ticht". The Bothy Loon, with his unfailingly cheerful smile, usually shakes his head and declares that "Naebody in the bothy ever wore onythin' like that," and the Fitba Loon just looks and nine times out of ten says, "Na, it's jist no me."

Father Bear, as I've probably said before, hates shopping, but one Christmas he came with me (very reluctantly) when I went to buy a new dress. Well, before he went off to park the car, I pointed out the place I was heading for and said I'd see him shortly. However, when I went inside and realised that the department I wanted was upstairs, I asked the downstairs assistant to keep an eye open for him. "And what does your husband look like?" she enquired. "Well," I replied. "If you see the picture of misery wearing a fawn duffle coat, that'll be him." She ushered him upstairs two minutes later!

Mind you, I should be used to all this carry on, for my father was exactly the same and as he spent most of his life working among black faced sheep, his clothing was often ripped to bits. One day when he was coming down the road from the dipper, he met a couple of local ladies who were out for a walk. "D'ye ken this," he said when he arrived home, "Ma breeks were in sic a state that I didnae ken whither tae walk forrit or backarts away frae thae twa weemin." Mother was black affrontit.

Anyway, I'm no longer black affrontit at the state of our 'milk hoose' and guess what I found? Two jackets, two pairs of waterproof leggings, a fleecy waistcoat and a boiler suit. And were there any more 'dusters?' No, not a single one.

* * *

Motors On The Mind

I've had some right daft dreams in my time, but the one I had a fortnight ago really took the biscuit. I was tearing along a little country road inside a big, empty shopping trolley, and every so often I had to stop and get help to manoeuvre it through folks' garden gates and things. "An' did it hae an engine in it then?" enquired Father Bear at breakfast time. "No," I replied, "it didn't." "So how did it manage tae go then?" he asked. "I don't know," I answered, "it just did."

Now, I'm quite sure that to anyone who can interpret dreams, this nonsense will probably reveal a great deal about my innermost feelings, but to me it's more than likely that I'd been wondering how I'd get around if Jessie failed her M.O.T. the following morning.

She was looking well, too, because Father Bear had instructed the Fitba Loon to give her a really good clean as he was half thinking of getting rid of her. However, after a two hour valeting, he changed his mind. "Ye ken this," said the Loon indignantly, "he'd nae intention o' sellin' that bloomin' car, he only said that so's I'd mak a really good job."

Well sadly, "Fine feathers don't make fine birds" and poor Jessie was given the thumbs down. As she set off for two days in the garage I thought.....no wonder I was dreaming about driving around in a shopping trolley,-anything would be preferable to our little red wagon, which is even more draughty than that thing the Flinstones drive around in.

My mother often said that she could write a book about old cars. Believe me, so could I.

You see, because we lived away up in a glen we really needed a car, but, as Father could only afford somebody else'e troubles, he just lurched from one breakdown to another. Possibly the most memorable escapade we had, though, was the time our ancient Daimler went on fire. Now this heap of decaying grandeur, which was probably around when the Titanic went down, had a very delicate column change gear stick and mother was always raging on about its fine mechanism being totally unsuited to such a coorse driver. Anyway, as we roared along the road that sour, drizzly December night, flames suddenly leaped up from the bonnet. Poor Mother began squealing like a bogey load of pigs hitting a pothole and father roared out "Dinnae panic!" as we careered up on to the grassy verge, where, to our everlasting gratitude, a young lad from a passing car appeared with a fire extinguisher.

"Here," announced father about half an hour later, "things is no sae bad efter a'...the R.A.F.'s commin' tae tak us hame." I sat silently in the back of the freezing car listening to mother ranting on about pigs in pokes and dugs that wid hae mair sense, and so on.

When I married Father Bear he had a wonderful black and yellow T.R.6 and as we zoomed along the roads in our high powered wasp I felt like a film star.

Three months and 5,000 laying hens later, the wasp had been replaced by an elderly diesel transit van which belched out black reek in all directions, broke down at traffic lights and was subjected to "routine police checks."

However, as the years passed our vehicle situation improved greatly and I'd almost forgotton what tantrums were until the little red wagon was born. Father Bear lovingly reconstructed its ancient "N" reg body into a jazzy, self important little workhorse which he then painted red, and blue and green.

Now, this vehicle detests me (the feeling's mutual) and one dark night its rancour sank to an all time low. I'd been at a kirk meeting, and as I picked my lonely way past the silent graveyard and in through the eerie sighing trees of the car park, my ears picked up a soft, unearthly sound. Wwoo - Wwoo, Wwoo - Wwoo. The weird, rasping sound grew louder with every step ....was this another Kirk Alloway? My heart nearly stopped when the awful truth dawned on me......the ghostly goings on were coming from the little red wagon.....the windscreen wipers were scraping back and forwards non stop on the dry glass!

"Oh aye," said Father Bear, roaring and laughing, "Ye'd maybe slammed the door ower hard." A shopping trolley wouldn't have done that!

Swanning About In The Rape Field

"I thocht I telt yae tae chase thae beggars o' swans aff the rape field afore ye cam in for your denner," said Father Bear to the Fitba Loon. "But Ah did," muttered the loon indignantly as he munched up his boiled ham pieces. "Well, ah hate tae tell ye, but they're a' back again....they'll sune hae flattened aboot an acre o' the flamin' stuff wie thae great muckle feet o' theirs."

Now, this swan business started off with two, but at the last count there were 15 and as they glide gracefully across the field each morning with all the elegance of a Tall Ships Race, we're at a loss as to how to get rid of them.

I was daft enough to think that we'd never see them again after I'd done my spectacular, squawking spread eagle run across the field, but, as I approached them, they all drew up their haughty heads and looked scornfully at this flapping, green eejit who, inspite of belting 250 yards along the tramline, still hadn't managed to take off. At the last minute they decided that, as a gesture of pity, they would fly away, but by the time I'd heched and peched my way back to the house they'd returned.

"Swans," exclaimed the Bothy Loon enthusiastically during our weekly phone call. "Michty me! Surely that's an honour! We must be gauin' up in the world when we've got swans eatin' oor ile seed rape. Ye ken maist fowk just hae ordinary things like doos and rabbits and craws, but niwer swans. Wait 'til I tell the lads aboot this." "Aye, well," replied Father Bear, "while ye're daein that, see if ony o' yer lecturer mannies ken hoo tae get rid o' the bloomin things."

Now, what I can't understand in the first place, is why these birds have decided to spend their days working slowly through our crop like a line of tea pickers, when there's a loch full of titbits and pond weed less than a hundred yards away.

"Is that where they are!" said a surprised Park Ranger when I phoned and asked for his advice. "You know," he continued, "we wondered where they'd gone because we count them every day and there's only five left." He very kindly said he'd put down some food to entice them back and Father Bear left the tractor in the field in the forlorn hope of scaring them away, but they're not daft.

Another bird that's not daft is Fred The Pheasant, who joined us in October 1997 and quickly became a household name. Fred led a very solitary existance and we often took pity on the brave little brown figure battling up the stubble field against the sleety blasts of winter to reach the safety of our garden. Father Bear opened the door of the big grain shed every morning so that his feathered friend could have breakfast and folk who came in about to shoot geese and ducks and things went away with the words "Noo, for goodness sake dinnae shoot Fred" ringing in their ears.

Well, nobody did, and come the Spring, two wee wifies in light brown coats arrived in response to Fred's advertisement on the Lonely Hearts page. One of them had the dubious honour of becoming Mrs. Fred, and her companion scurried off home to have another look at the paper.

I wouldn't have said Fred was much of a family man, and it came as no great surprise when Mrs. Fred gathered the Fredettes together one fine August morning and disappeared without leaving a forwarding address.

Fred, who'd never really changed his spots, returned to being a carefree batchelor again and continued to pursue his usual solitary interests, but we're getting a bit concerned because we haven't seen him around for ages.

"Aye," said Father Bear the other day, "Ah doot the puir devil's had it. He's never bed awa this long afore. Ye ken, ye fair miss him."

But, that's just life, isn't it? We're anxiously waiting for one bird to reappear and at the same time, we're waiting for 2 dozen others to disappear.

However, things could be worse, for I was talking to a farmer's wife yesterday who told me that one of her neighbours has 50 swans on his rape this year. I haven't told Father Bear or the Fitba Loon because this farm's only five miles away.....as the crow flies!

* * *

Fags Vow More Than Food For Thought

In case you didn't see it on the nine o' clock news ...... Father Bear has given up smoking.

Now this has nothing to do with the recent 'National No Smoking Day', because he isn't into community martyrdom. (It's far better to suffer alone). It had more to do with me not buying him cigarettes because he'd already puffed his way through the weekly quota.

A friend we were visiting that Saturday asked if he'd stopped smoking. "No," growled Father Bear. "She never bocht me ony, did she!" And then he turned down the kind offer of a cigar, saying ...... "Na, na, it's a' richt thanks. A'll dae withoot."

Well, he did, and although he was like a bear with a burnt tail for the rest of the day he didn't give in. Every time he went into the kitchen to rummage for food, he glanced hopefully at the space on the shelf beside the mug which plays "Fitba' Crazy," but the fag fairies had forgotten him.

By tea time he could have eaten three horses and a dungspreader and long before supper time he was on the prowl again for "something tasty."

"You know we should get one of those little ovens they have in bakers shops for keeping things warm and fill it up each morning with pies and sausage rolls," I said. "Oh here," he said enthusiastically, "now there's an idea. Y'see, if there wis stuff like that tae eat I wouldnae need chocolate biscuits an' crisps, because they're awfy fattenin', I'll be like the back end o' a hoose in nae time if I'm no smokin'. Mind that's what happened afore."

As you'll now have gathered, this is not the first time he's made an effort

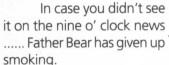

to give up the weed, and a few years back, he managed to keep off it for 15 months, but he put on weight and moaned constantly about his nose and throat being sore.

"Ye ken," he said, coughing contentedly through a thick cloud of reek (after the New Year's socialising had seen his resolution go up in smoke), "Ah'm feelin' far better noo that Ah'm back on the fags again!"

I suppose I really should have more sympathy towards

folk who are trying to give up smoking, but when I was a teenager I had to listen to mother's never ending tirade about the evils of smoking and drinking, and alas, in those distant, poorer than a church mouse days of Rock 'n' Roll, I could barely afford a cheap lipstick, let alone the forbidden fruit.

However, before you get the impression that I'm a right little Goody Two Shoes, I'd better tell you that I'm a self confessed choc-a-holic. Chocolate is my weakness and I could eat the stuff to a band playing. Bars, biscuits, boxes, buttons ......the lot, but with a famishing Father Bear looting my supplies, a chocolate war is about to blow up.

Talking of blow ups takes me back to the time that Bruin Two (The Troot Fisher) brought home a packet of tiny cigarette bombs from a trick shop. While we all sat around the living room trying to look casual, Father Bear puffed away good style behind his newspaper, totally unaware that the King size, which had been a fraction out of line with the others in the packet, had been doctored with an explosive no bigger than a sliver of grass.

Well, we certainly got our money's worth. The instant the bang went off, he leapt from his chair like a scalded cat. The pages of the newspaper crashed to the floor. The cigarette went flying across the room and his tongue, (which he was mighty relieved to find was still there) came away with some of the most colourful adjectives we'd ever heard!

Anyway, Braveheart's daily raids are still continuing. He hasn't (as far as we know) surrendered to the enemy and although he was given a couple of patches by The Salmon Fisher, (Bruin One's well meaning husband who's also stopped smoking) he only kept them on for ten minutes. "They were awfy itchy an' onyway, I dinnae want tae become addicted tae thae things as weel as fags."

And, now for the bit that really takes the biscuit. When he collected me from a meeting the other night his very first words were....."Phuw! Ye're fair stinkin' o' cigarettes. Ye've surely been in among a richt crowd o' smokers the nicht."

Just Another One Of Those Not-So-Restful Days

"Time and tide wait for no man" and when the alarm ripped through the silent house at 5.00 a.m. last Monday I just knew it was to be 'another one of those days'.

Father Bear had to be away early with his tractor and bogie to unload a fertiliser boat at the docks and his nose bag was fair bulging with pieces, chocolate biscuits, cakes, crisps, coke and a big flask of coffee. (I wonder if Desperate Dan ever stopped smoking.) As he hurried away into the morning mist, his parting words were...."Noo, see'n keep look'n in on the chickens every wee while an' get the loon tae shoo thae beggars o' swans aff the ile seed rape."

A bemused Buffy, who'd been scuttering about among our feet wondering why we were having our breakfast when she wasn't even hungry, disappeared for another bit of shuteye and the Fitba' Loon, who'd gone into injury time the previous Thursday, was still sound asleep. (He dislocated a bone in his back when the fence post he'd been yanking out snapped and catapulted him head first into a bed of thistles). He wasn't singing "Flower of Scotland" that day, I can tell you!

Well, I went back to bed, but I couldn't sleep for worrying about the chickens and so, ten minutes later I was shuffling across the close in a huge droopy boiler suit and a pair of wellies with treads like tractor tyres, looking for all the world like a penguin running for a fish supper.

After I'd spent about an hour wandering slowly through my big, smelly, six week old feathered friends (they're not cute and fluffy any more) and removing any dead ones, I had a look at the awesome array of high-tech controls which were clickin' and flickin' away goodstyle on the wall. The temperature was hovering around 20°C. The moisture was 70% and I didn't need a computer to tell me that nobody would have sat beside me on a bus.

"Dad 'phoned when you were out," announced the Fitba' Loon, "an' he's needin' a starter switch for the tractor.......Well, I think that's what he wants onyway. But ye'd better listen tae the message yersel." (Judging by the background noise the Q.E.2 must have been berthing alongside the bogie.)

Oh well, I sighed, I may as well go and get it over and done with, but, as the car began to warm up on the twelve mile trip, I was wishing I'd changed out of my foul smelling clothes. A female country singer was crying her heart out on the car tape about how she was lookin' for freedom and nobody seemed to care. Sister, I thought, I know exactly how you feel.

I was hardly back in the house again when the doorbell rang. "One of your horses is stuck in the fence," said a worried mannie. As I struggled into the early morning glamour again and headed down south with an apple in my pocket I thought...........it's o.k. for some, away playing with bloomin' boats at the seaside!

Now, this horse and his two sidekicks only lodge with us and I never see them from one week to the next, but of course this was the old Sod's Law situation again, wasn't it.?

Stuck was an understatement. This beast was totally wedged between his shelter shed and a barbed wire fence and even if I'd gone up and shouted 'knackery' in his ear he couldn't have done much about it.

Eventually, after much pushing and shoving and coaxing he got the message and to our great relief (his and mine), he very gingerly reversed out of his predicament.....But, there was no way that he would let his two envious pals get even the tiniest scrap of his apple.

By mid afternoon the loon was so fed up of the swans ("There's 30 o' them noo") that I took the old stunt kite down to the field to see if that might scare them away.

I was over the moon when they flew off in terror at the sight of it soaring in the sky, but, pride goeth before a fall and seconds later the stupid thing took a great nose dive on to the corrugated roof of the horses shelter and disintegrated.

"Whit a day it's been," said Father Bear, "Ye ken, I've never stoppit. Are the chickens a' richt?"

HUH!

* * *

Sight of Cat Basket Gives Game Away

Last week Buffy the cat lost her voice and her appetite and her oomph. Well, to be honest, she really doesn't have much oomph nowadays, but she was looking that pathetic we decided she'd better go and see her doctor.

Now, as you will maybe have noticed, when your four legged friend gets wind of this visit it often disappears (or gey near flips its lid, like the dog in Billy Connelly's song D.I.V.O.R.C.E.) and it's not the first time I've had to make an apologetic phone call to the vet's surgery with the news that his 3.15. patient was last spotted over an hour ago, belting down the field towards the wood.

Of course, we never mentioned the word to Buffy, but the minute she spotted the cat basket, that was it....she managed to get into reverse and apply the brakes at the same time. However, The Fitba' Loon came to my rescue and 30 seconds later, after a very undignified struggle, her dishevelled face with its bent whiskers glowered out at us through the plastic portcullis.

Mind you, these modern pet boxes are wonderful things. I still have vivid memories of the days I humped cats about in cardboard boxes tied with binder twine and before the car was at the end of the farm road the beggars were usually running around daft in the back window yowling their heads off.

My worst experience of that, was the time that Big Angus clawed his way out of the box and wedged himself under the driving seat of the car. He just wouldn't budge and I had to go and tell the vet that his next patient was refusing to come in. "Come on, come on son," pleaded the young vet, "out you come, there's a lad." The 'lad' had no intention of doing any such thing and the next five minutes seemed like an eternity as I stood there, not knowing whether to laugh or greet.

Father Bear, however, had the daddy of all 'cat'astrophes.

One grey winter's afternoon when I was returning home from school with the two young Bruins we saw him standing half submerged in a ditch about a hundred yards from the house and he seemed to be waving very enthusiastically. We waved back just as enthusiastically, but we kept going.

About ten minutes later I thought I could hear somebody shouting and when I looked out the front door I realised it was Father Bear's voice.

What a reception I got. He hadn't moved from the spot and he was clutching the tail of a big ferocious looking cat which was jerking up and down like a yo-yo on a knotted string.

"Surely ye micht hae kent I wisnae jist wavin' tae ye," he ranted. "Did ye no realise there was something wrang? Ah've been stuck here for nearly half an 'oor an' ah'm jist aboot clawed tae daith wie this beggar.........look, it even sank its teeth intae the tae o' ma boot." "Come and gie's a hand tae get this trap aff the puir devil's front leg." Well, it turned out the 'puir devil,' who must have dragged the trap for miles, was practically wild, but we felt he deserved a chance so, a month later, thanks to the vet's skill and a bit of home nursing, Growler, as we called him, hit the lonely trail again on three and a half legs. We would have kept him but sadly, he was a travellin' man.

I'm sure people think I'm a bit odd when I say that I enjoy my visits to the vet, but I do. Oh, we've had our sad times, just like everybody else, but the place has a very busy, happy atmosphere and you couldn't meet a kindlier bunch of folk. And then, of course, there's the not to be missed, impromptu floor show of baskets and boxes etc., sitting hissing and growling at each other as they await their turn.

Well, Buffy, after all the hoo-haa she kicked up, turned into the model patient as soon as she was on the examination table. She sat there as if somebody had knitted her and then, after her consultation was over, she walked meekly into her detested box again and lay down. When we returned home, one emerged unruffled and regal and walked grandly to one's dish with a sniff and a disdainful flick of one's tail. It's so typical, isn't it?

* * *

Courgette Creation Puts Fitba Loon's Mother In The Soup

"Cream of courgette soup and ingins," echoed the Fitba Loon in disgust. "Aw yuk, I hate thae cucumbery things an' ye ken fine Ah dinnae like ingins." "Hiv ye nuthin' else?" "A tin o' tamatie or something." "No I don't," I replied crossly, "but it's good, and it tastes quite like leek and tattie."

"Whit!! How can it taste like leek and tattie if it's made wie courgettes?" (His question reminded me of that T.V. ad. where the two lads drove around the countryside in their wee morris minor wondering how 'the wife' was clever enough to make pea and ham soup frae a chicken.)

Needless to say, Father Bear's comments didn't exactly make it recipe of the week either when he said ..... "Aye well, it's kinda needin somethin' else in it..... dae ye no' think?..... Ye ken whit a mean?" "Oh, I know fine what you mean," I replied in exasperation.

Delia Smith would still be working on "101 Ways With Ham and Eggs" if she had a husband like mine.

Do you know that less than a week ago he informed me that he's never liked fish cakes. "But I've been making you fish cakes for nearly 23 years and you've never complained til' now," I exclaimed in astonishment. "Aye well," he replied, "we dinnae really hae them that often, so I've aye just eaten them, like. Ah've never enjoyed them though!" Mind you, he's always made a fuss about 'maybe' getting a fish bone stuck in his throat' when we have fish, even although I've reassured him that I've gone through the blinking stuff with a fine tooth comb. "Aye," chipped in the Bothy Loon, "but look at The Queen Mither .... Ah'll bet ye that's whit fowk telt her as weel." Do you know that one morning he even had the neck to say that Big Angus (the cat) was better fed than him. So I thought, 'Right chum, we'll soon see about that! Well, when teatime came he glowered at the elaborately garnished plate of salad which I set down in front of him and said "What on earth is that!" (well, to be honest, those weren't his exact words.) "It's salad," I replied with a straight face. "I ken fine it's salad," he replied, screwing up his face, "but what's that smelly broon stuff in the middle, an' a' thae wee hard lookin' roond things on the cocktail sticks?" "Oh," I said casually, "that's

Angus's tea.....he fair enjoyed your pork pie and roast beef!"

Now, I wouldn't have said Father Bear really appreciated this joke (even when I produced his own plate) but everyone else did.......especially Grandfather Bear. He never ever complains about what I give him and he says "They're a' far ower bloomin' fussy onywey." But then he knew what it was like to live in the days when brose was the staple diet and a teuch auld hen was a treat.

Our modern Bothy Loon has concocted his own version of brose, but he's keeping the recipe under his 'mealer' for the time being. However, I can tell you what the ingredients are because I have to buy them when he's at home. Porridge oats......(see'n get the packet wie the mannie in the kilt). Red grape juice, (nae green). A bag o' raisins, (nivver sultannas) an' a puckle purple grapes (but green anes'll dae if that's a' they've got). If Grandfather Bear saw this concoction he would say "It's enough tae blaw yer bannet aff."

Of course, after bringing up four of a family and feeding the proverbial 5,000 forbye, I'm well used to folks' likes and dislikes.

Offals are top of the thumbs down list. Liver, kidney, tongue and of course the dreaded tripe......."That's that disgusting stuff that looks like lumps o' wet nappies!"

Poor old mince come next ("She thinks if she pits some curry and raisins in it we'll no ken it's mince") and "Spew Stew"......well that's about as welcome as bluebottle in a plate of semolina.

However, over the years I've had my share of compliments and, without a doubt, the most memorable of those was when I said to the mother of a young lad who was working for us, that her son ate whatever I put down in front of him. "Oh aye," she replied, "he's never been fussy, he'll eat onything!"

He'd have eaten my courgette soup!

* * *

Tobacco Reek Tale — A Festival Highlight

The merciless fingers of the mountain wind tore at my clothes and my hair as I clambered up the slope to "pit a steen on the cairn" at the top of the Cairn o' Mount and I shouted across the bleak, barren, brown moorland to the Bothy Loon that I must be needing my head examined.

"Na, na, Mither," came the Loon's windswept words as his faded tartan shirt flapped against his slim frame. "Ye cannae pass the cairn and nae pit a steen on it. I mean it's bound tae be unlucky or something. Dae ye no think?"

Think! I'd done nothing but think the whole blinkin' day. You see, Father Bear and the Fitba' Loon weren't coming up north with us to the folk festival. They were spending their weekend at home cleaning out the chicken shed and that meant I'd been tearin' around all day (like a bloomin' moose at a threshing mill), trying to make everything as easy as possible for them while I was away.

"Now listen," I said to Father Bear, after I'd done the tea dishes and tidied up the kitchen, "I've left two lists of instructions on the top of the cooker. One is for the two of you and the other is for Buffy.......and remember, she'll not eat her food if her dish is dirty!" "Aye, aye, nae bother, we'll manage fine," he assured me (with one eye on the television). "Dinnae worry yer heid aboot us. If we dinnae like the look o' the stuff ye've left in the fridge we'll jist gae in for fish suppers an' things. See'n enjoy yersels. When'll ye be back?"

We drove round by the chicken shed to say cheerio to the Fitba' Loon and when I mentioned to him that I'd set the washing machine in case he felt like washing any of his smelly chicken clothes his look of pure disbelief made me feel I was making about as much sense as the Teletubbies.

However, as we headed on up country, I began to relax and join in with the Bothy Loon as he practised his songs for the weekend. The lady who arranges the accommodation for all the guest singers and musicians was telling me that when he returned his acceptance form stating his requirements, he said he needed "A bed for masel. Ane for ma mither an' a gless o' water for her false teeth!"

I had a great time and I thoroughly enjoyed everything from the long, leisurely breakfasts, right through to the wonderful singarounds which lasted well into the wee sma' 'oors. I bumped into the Bothy Loon from time to time, but there was another singer that I was looking out for.....a local lad, who, according to Father Bear, could tell me why he, our alleged non smoker, came home from a recent agricultural show reekin' of cigarettes...... (among other things).

"Here!" I said, when I eventually caught up with him. "I've a bone to pick with you".............. "Now," he interupted (and held up both his hands like we used to do when we were playing at Cowboys and Indians). "Afore ye say onything, it had nothing whatsoever tae dae wie me. He jist happened tae be standin' next tae me when I wis smokin' and that's how he cam hame smellin' o' fags!" And I'm the one who's supposed to be the prizewinning storyteller!

MInd you, between ourselves, I knew fine Father bear had been puffing away on the fly before ever he went near the show.

Well, sadly, Sunday evening came round all too soon and after we'd bid farewell to everyone, it was time to take the road south again.

The Cairn o' Mount was lonely and spooky and still as I dutifully trotted up the slope with my wee chuckie and by the time we arrived home it was nearly dark.

The place looked real tidy, apart from one or two take-away dishes and Father Bear listened with great interest to all our news.

Halfheartedly, I asked him and the Fitba' Loon, who was engrossed in the television, if they wanted any supper. "Oh aye," they chorused, "that wid be nice."

Isn't it lovely to be appreciated!

* * *

Musings On Modified Berries

We'll soon be into strawberry season again, but never mind, the days of sluggy, fly ridden berries mouldering away on damp ground could soon be a thing of the past if plans to genetically modify them are successful.

You see, I was reading in the paper that some researchers are proposing to carry out a field trial to see if it's possible to produce a berry which will not only look and taste better, but will be more resistant to damage and moulds.

Now, I haven't done botany and biology since the dinosaurs were busy knockin' lumps out out of each other, but I've tried to imagine what might happen if proposals to introduce genes from kiwi fruit, barley, yeast and cow beans go ahead.

The mention of cow beans made me wonder if they could be the same variety that Jack and The Beanstalk's mother flung out of the window in disgust after he arrived home and admitted he'd swapped them for a cow, en route to the market. (Mind you, he's not the first lad to find himself in the dog house after a day at the market. Is he?)

If they are, then isn't it possible that the genes from these giant beans could result in the strawberries of the future growing on trees instead of sprawling all over the ground and the Kiwi genes - well, they could maybe act as a skin toughener to prevent all the slugs and creepie crawlies from having a field day.

You can just picture them trailing across the garden to the strawberry patch and finding that their gums are bouncing off the new breed of berries. It would be like the terrible advertisement for frozen vegetables that used to be on television, where only the smallest, sweetest vegetables were allowed into the frozen food factory, and all the rejects were standing on the other side of the fence roarin' an' greetin'. It was enough to put you off buying the stuff.

Yeast always conjures up a picture of little fat cottage loaves sitting in a warm place slowly doubling their size and so, I could see all the little strawberries growing twice as big as they hung around in the warm sunshine.

Here, I thought, this 'G.M.' business has endless possibilities.

I couldn't however, seem to find an obvious use for the barley, and when I said jokingly to the Fitba Loon, (who'd come in for the car keys and was squinting over my shoulder) that the barley was the last straw, he slowly replied "Aye, so's yer stories aboot thae strawberries."

"Are they as bad as that? ....D'ye think I should start again?"....."Na na," he answered, shaking his head. "Ye may as weel keep gaun,' ye couldnae get ony worse."

He shakes his head in despair over my attempts at jokes, and one afternoon when I was taking him to a match, we passed a lorry load of sheep. "Is that your supporters bus?" I asked. He looked out of the side window so that I couldn't see the smirk on his face and replied......."Ah dinnae ken why ye jist dinnae gie up!"

That was what he usually did in the distant days when I used to drag him and the Bothy Loon along to some P.Y.O. place for jam strawberries. The pair of them would be fine for a wee while and then it would start. "Mum, he's not picking any berries" .... "But I'm needing the toilet".............."You went to the toilet before you left"......"But, I'm needing again..........and there's a funny lookin' wee green beastie on my leg."

I often wondered why I bothered. I'd have been cheaper and less harassed at the end of the day buying the bloomin' jam. But my mother would never have forgiven me. I can remember her standing in front of the old cooker for hours on end .... with a hairnet on......making hers, and Bruin One, the nurse, thought she was in seventh heaven when gran allowed her to put on the jampot covers.

Anyway, none of us can tell what lies ahead, but maybe someday, when we're picking fruit the size of apples from shady, overhanging branches, we'll look back with nostalgia to the strawberry fields of long ago.

* * *

The Perils Of Living Close By

We've always been blessed with good neighbours and when the family who lived in the little white house beside the oilseed rape field flitted into the town a few weeks ago, we were real sorry to see them go.

Now, what these long suffering souls put up with over the seven years they lived here would make the Neighbours from Hell seem like a bunch of pussycats and I really think they deserve some sort of an award or other in the New Years Honours list. Possibly the Order Of The Bath.....just to remind them of the many times they couldn't get theirs filled because Father Bear had dug up their water supply.

Of course, he never meant to. It's just that he seems to have this divine ability to locate water mains ..... anywhere and everywhere ..... in fact, I wouldn't even let him loose in the Sahara Desert with a digger.

I can still remember the cold winter's morning that he came tearing in to the kitchen and said "Ye ken that plastic pipe I dug up the other day ......the ane that gangs doon tae the twa hooses .....well, it must hae been richt hard frost last nicht for the bloomin' thing's frozen solid."

"Look," I said (and I was really fizzin') "These folk have a young baby and the last thing they need is to be without water. What are you going to do about it?" Talk about asking a stupid question. Five minutes later the pair of us were running up and down what seemed like a mile of piping with pots and kettles of warm water trying to thaw the blasted thing out.

Of course it wasn't just the lack of water they had to contend with. Every time we were installing electrical things (and especially when the big chicken shed was going up) they had no power either. It was just a good job that Granny and Grandad lived nearby.

Then there were the days they phoned and told us they'd a horse looking in their window, or a few sheep admiring their lawn. Their sense of humour, fortunately, was second to none and when they heard that one of "their sheep" had taken a Saturday afternoon stroll into town and landed up in custodial grass at the ba-a-a-ck of the local police station for allegedly disturbing the peace and loitering with intent, they just about died laughing.

But, it didn't end there, good gracious, no. They'd been stunk out by broiler dung, reeked out by strawburning, covered in thick brown stoor off the fields and wakened up at all hours with heavy machinery trundling past and folk shooting vermin.

Our other neighbours, who live in the little brown house a wee bit further down the road, haven't suffered quite so much, but one day, they were a bit taken aback by a rather unexpected outburst from Father Bear, who'd gone down to inspect The Fitba Loon's ploughing in the corner of the field adjacent to their high, cupress hedge.

"Whit a blooming mess ye're makin o' that" he ranted. "ye've dug doon far ower deep and jist brocht up a' the rubbish o' the day. Whit'n earth were ye thinkin' aboot? Ye're surely no expecting' onythin' tae grow in that, are ye?" (or words to that effect).

He was very taken aback when, in the ensuing silence, a quiet, feminine voice from behind the hedge said ..... "I hope you're not meaning me!" ..... She'd been planting bulbs.

Well, I'm very happy to say that we have yet again been blessed with good neighbours in the little white house beside the oilseed rape field and when they came up to introduce themselves, we had a good crack over a cup of tea and a bite of supper. However, for me the real icebreaker of the visit was when their very well behaved dog nipped discreetly back into the house and polished off the last piece of sponge cake, while his family were up seeing the chickens.

I laughingly brushed aside their embarrassed apologies, because I knew exactly how they felt ..... I've been apologising for Father Bear's escapades for years.

Ailing Combines Are The Last Straw For Father Bear

Do you remember the happy-go-lucky, wonderfully cheerful, straw-chewin' Wurzels who shot up the charts with their bouncy song ..... "I Got A Brand New Combine Harvester?" Well, at the moment Father Bear's got the flipside of that catchy little number......"I Got A Clapped Out Combine Harvester." In fact, it's even worse than that ......he's got two.

Do you know this, what with all the hammering and grinding and welding that's been going on over the past few weeks it's been like living next door to the Q.E.2 being built and I just can't wait for the day that these two yellow giants come sailing out of the big shed with their unmistakable, high powered whine and roar off into the noonday sun.

Our mealtime conversations (if you could call them that) are full of wearisome words like drum, bubble-auger, concave, spool-valve, chopper, shakers, bearings, belts, riddles and headers, and Father Bear, who's permanently covered in grease from head to toe, is about as approachable as a Rottweiler with a gumboil.

"Jist come oot an' see whit they're askin' 30 quid for," he said the other morning. I went out and looked at this inoffensive little piece of metal leaning against the wall and tut tutted. "Ye ken," he went on, "it's jist an absolute scandal what they're expectin' fowk tae fork oot nooadays. The hale thing's jist a bloomin' rip aff. Ye ken that's the price o' half a ton o' barley.......that's whit fowk dinnae realise."

While we were standing there, the Fitba' Loon plodded silently by with a huge roll of cable over his shoulder, looking as if he'd just let in 20 goals at Hampden and a crowd of doos flew over the steading enroute to the oilseed rape field. Life, I thought to myself, is just one great big bowl of cherries.

But the combines are not the only things that are needing sorted. Dear me no. The swather's sitting grinning from ear to ear (dear knows why) the little red wagon failed its M.O.T. (deliberately, no doubt) and although Grandfather Bear's faithful wee car did its best, it didn't pass either.

I think there was a lot to be said for the days of scythes and binders. I mean there was a limit to what could break down, wasn't there? I can remember my father and uncle sweating and swearing in the hot September sun over a binder that kept choking and breaking down, but I've often wondered how the pair of them would have coped with a combine.....it would have been like something out of Laurel and Hardy.

One afternoon, a few years back, I asked Grandfather Bear if he could make me a couple of sheaves for a local harvest festival. Without further ado, he set off with his trusty scythe over his shoulder to the field which was being combined. Well, by the time he arrived there, the combine had gone on fire and when a short tempered and harassed Father Bear spotted the familiar figure striding across the field with the scythe, he immediately jumped to the wrong conclusion and shouted to the lad that was helping him. "Wid ye jist tak a look at that! Here's that stupid auld goat comin' wi that flamin' scythe o' his. Does he think he's bloomin' Superman or something?".....(Wee Baby Bear's other Grandad thought this was just the best harvest story he'd heard in ages.)

However, things looked up a bit at the weekend, because, as the machinery parts Father Bear was needing still hadn't been delivered, work came to a bit of a standstill. The Fitba Loon shot off to his Saturday match and his five-a-side Sunday Tournament and his father wandered about like something in an enclosure at the zoo.

Suddenly he said......"How dae ye fancy gae'n for a walk?" A Walk! I couldn't believe my ears. We never go for a walk. "Where to?" I asked. "Well" he replied, "If ye pit on yer wellies we'll hae a wander doon the tramlines in the barley field an pu' oot the wild oats."

Who said romance is dead!

* * *

Fond Memories Of Past Glorious Twelfths

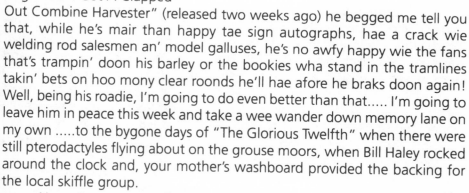

Due to the phenomenal succes of Father Bear's single ....."I Got A Clapped Out Combine Harvester" (released two weeks ago) he begged me tell you that, while he's mair than happy tae sign autographs, hae a crack wie welding rod salesmen an' model galluses, he's no awfy happy wie the fans that's trampin' doon his barley or the bookies wha stand in the tramlines takin' bets on hoo mony clear roonds he'll hae afore he braks doon again! Well, being his roadie, I'm going to do even better than that..... I'm going to leave him in peace this week and take a wee wander down memory lane on my own .....to the bygone days of "The Glorious Twelfth" when there were still pterodactyles flying about on the grouse moors, when Bill Haley rocked around the clock and, your mother's washboard provided the backing for the local skiffle group.

Now, I've never really had any interest in shooting (or hunting or fishing) and although they're very emotive subjects nowadays, to me, a teenager living up a highland glen, grouse-beating for the local Laird was simply a way of earning a bit of money to buy new school clothes and other odds and ends a deputy sheepdog's pay didn't run to.

Before the great day arrived, I always went down to the big wood beside the river to cut myself a sturdy hazel stick on which I'd carefully carve my name .... A good stick was worth its weight in gold, because as well as serving as a flagpole, it often had to be used for vaulting over peat-bogs and deep ditches and........adders.

I can still remember that ripening August morning. There I was, a real eager beaver, standing at the top of our close waiting for my transport to arrive ....my stick in one hand and my old, scuffed school bag (bulging with boring blackcurrant jam pieces, a bottle of lemonade and a pair of father's socks) in the other.

And what a squash! When the old estate lorry shuddered to a standstill, it was overflowing with gamekeepers, beaters, dogs, piecebags and sticks and while I was being hauled unceremoniously up into the back, my face was licked enthusiastically by a big slavery spotted spaniel with bad breath, which then sat and whined in my ear for the rest of the bumpy journey.

Well, it seemed a bit of a dawdle for a pound a day, but, as the month wore on, the terrain grew steeper and the burns gouged deeper. I tore my tough jeans as I slithered down the steep scree slopes of my first Munro. I became totally disorientated in acres of six foot high bracken, I dined on cranberries, I cheered with my sidekicks when the shooters missed and I clapped loudly when a retriever ran through the burn dragging the big bag of cartridges that somebody had thoughtlessly hung round its neck.

And we came across some unexpected sights too. One day, far far away from civilisation, as around 30 of us poured over the edge of a high ridge, we spotted, in the river valley away down below, an encampment of soldiers who'd dispensed with their clothing and were splashing around in the shallow, sunlit water. Suddenly, they became aware of this noisy, flag waving, wolf whistling crowd of folk streaming down the steep hillside and I have never, ever, seen a group of men beat such a hasty retreat.

I haven't forgotten the caterpillar either. It lay in state in a plate of mince and tatties and cabbage the day our gamekeeper's wife gave me my dinner. The sight of its bleached body nearly turned my stomach, but as I couldn't face eating it, and to save her from being black affrontit, I discreetly made it a cabbage shroud and left it lying under my knife.

Oh dear, I'll have to go. Father Bear has just been on the phone..... "Ah'm needin' a 13mm Ratchett spanner and the long clatt"..... Who'd be a roadie?

Now, where did I see that advert for Grouse Beaters!

* * *

Taking The Easy Way Out
- The Best Laid Plans

"That field o' oilseed rape's jist no quite ready for swathin' .....it's fell green in places, Ah'll maybe better gie it anither day or twa yit," said Father Bear, the other Saturday afternoon.

"Oh good," I replied, "does that mean we can all go out somewhere for our tea?"

"Ah'm no really awfy hungry the noo," he stated as he lowered himself down into the chair opposite me in the porch. "I micht feel like somethin' later on though." He never seems to realise that I get sick fed up of making pieces and cooking,.....day in, day out.

"Whaur wis ye thinkin' on gaun onywey?" he enquired, flicking through the newspaper he'd picked up. Before I'd time to reply, the Bothy Loon came striding through, grease up to the elbows and I repeated my question. "Oh well, ah dinnae ken aboot that, though. Ye see, ah'm reconstructin' the auld mower for the millennium, and ah'm nae feenished yet." (Grandfather Bear and the wee fergie used to spend half their summer scurrying over rape field stubbles and along grass verges with this famous 'mower' puttering on behind). "Ah'm nae really fussed either wey. Ah'd be quite happy wie a plate o' salad."

Five minutes later the Fitba Loon arrived home from the match, all smiles and, parrot like, I repeated the question yet again.

"Whaur tae, like?" he asked and when I said, "just the usual place," his face lit up. "Aye O.K. Whit time though? Ye see, it's my turn tae drive the lads tae the disco the nicht and ah'll hae tae be oot o' here afore eight......An' ah'll need the car, because we'll a' hae on wir guid claes."

Things, I thought, are getting better by the minute.

"Right," I said, decisively. "I'm going to phone up and see if we can get an early booking." "Oh," replied the lady, in a very apologetic voice, "I'm afraid we don't start serving until 7.30 p.m. and .....we're fully booked tonight. I'm sorry." So was I!

Now, it goes without saying that none of the others were very disappointed at this news and Father Bear said, "Ye ken, ah fair fancy a fish supper."

"Right," I replied, resigning myself to the inevitable. "Who wants what?"

"Aye, ah'll hae a dressed fish supper," announced Father Bear. (I always have this picture of a fish standing in a tail coat with a red carnation in its button hole and cufflinks in its white shirt.

"An ah'll jist hae some salad," announced the Bothy Loon.

"Could I maybe get twa chicken burgers and french fries," shouted the Fitba' Loon above the roar of his bath water. As I drove into town I thought, well, I suppose this is still easier than making the tea. First, I parked the car beside the wee supermarket and after I'd bought the Bothy Loon's salad stuff, I went across the street to our favourite chippy. But that's when things began to go wrong, because was it not shut for the bloomin' holidays?

Well, I drove a couple of hundred yards down the street to the next one. But when I stepped inside the door, the twenty or so folk, who were packed into the place like sardines, gave me a glassy stare as I turned and walked out again.

Why is life like this, I thought as I headed off in the car to chippy number three.

But, there wasn't a blinkin' parking space for miles, was there, so, I ended up at chippy number four.

"Can I have two breaded fish suppers please," I asked when it eventually came to my turn. "Sorry hen, nae breaded fish, jist battered fish." Battered, I fumed, there'll be more than the fish battered tonight!

As I pulled into the drive through bit for the Fitba' Loon's burgers and french fries I could feel 'cairry-oot' rage coming on, because there were eight cars in front of me and when I arrived home (nearly an hour later and not in the best of humour) I was just waiting for a comment like....."Wis Glescae busy the day?"

However, no-one uttered a cheep, until the Bothy Loon said......"Well, Mither, ye've ha'en a fine, easy tea the nicht. Hivn't ye!"

* * *

All In A Farmer's Wife's Weekend

It was a lovely, sunny Saturday morning with an Autumn nip in the air when I drove the Fitba' Loon the twenty or so miles to the docks to finish unloading the fertiliser boat he'd been working on the previous day.

"Ah should be back in time for the hame game this efternane," he said, as he went off to bring his tractor and bogie out of one of the big storage sheds, but, he added wistfully "Ah wid hae richt liket tae hae gone tae Ibrox the day."

When I arrived home, at the back of eight, the place was going like a fair. A grain lorry was being loaded. Another lorry was unloading lime. The close was full of vehicles and Father Bear was running round like a scalded cat.

Right, I thought, I'll away and make the next two lots of pieces and then I'll wash the dishes.

Needless to say, I had everything laid out on the kitchen table when Father Bear arrived in with two friends (and Jake the dog) for a cup of coffee. One of them was needing a combine driver and the other, who has come to our rescue many times, wondered if we were needing a hand.

Well, Father Bear's furrowed forehead worked out some sort of compromise or other and the three of them ....(and Jake)....eventually got up from the table and went away outside, still discussing headers and knives and horns and trolleys.

"Ah'm oot o' fags tae," shouted Father Bear over his shoulder.

"Oh you would be, " I snapped, "I suppose I'll have to go and get the blasted things ....This kitchen's like a pigsty!"

When I returned the 'phone was ringing. It was another fertiliser boat for the Fitba' Loon on Monday morning .....6.00am start.

I was heading upstairs to the toilet when the blinkin' thing rang again. "Aye, that's the bit in for yer combine," said the cheerful voice at the other end. "Right," I said, "thanks very much.....I'll be in for it in about ten minutes."

Before I left, I put the dishes in the sink to soak, but as I was driving off, the Bothy Loon came tearing over to the car and said. "Mither, could ye maybe get twa rolls o' edge tae edge net wrap when ye're in? Ah'm gaun awa tae a ferm doon near the coast an' Ah dinnae want tae run short."

Surely, I thought, when I arrived back yet again .....I'll get peace now to do the dishes and a couple of loads of washing ....

"Could ye come an' follow along ahent the combine wie the car.... the bloomin' indicators are no workin," announced a harassed Father Bear. "Of course I will," I replied sarcastically, "I've got nothing else to do anyway."

Well, this combine raced along the road with its rear end swaying from side to side like an enormous duck in a hurry. Several old ladies stood riveted to the pavement as we roared past them belching out clouds of stoor and barley awns and I felt quite sad as I spotted the Loons' Ibrox bus pulling away from the bus stop.

Sunday began the way it meant to continue and I was sent off on a 50 miles round trip for a coupling block and plunger for one of the combines..... "An' ye'll maybe bring anither twa rolls o' edge tae edge net wrap while ye're there," shouted the Bothy Loon. When I returned I found he'd gone away without his piece bag. "Aye," he interrupted, when he heard my exasperated "hello" on his mobile phone, "Ah ken ah did."

Now, of course, apart from being nearly driven daft running about after three menfolk I still have "My" chickens to look after and before Father Bear left that morning he said "Noo, ye'll hae tae keep an eye on that water thing up in the shed, so come an' ah'll show ye whit tae dae."

After watching him very carefully I turned to him and said...."Is that all there is to it?....You know, monkeys could do that."

"Aye well," he replied. "Maybe they could, but, there's nae monkeys here the day, so you'll jist hae tae dae."

No wonder I look forward so much to my weekends!

Acknowledgements
I would like to acknowledge the sources of the material quoted in the earlier pages of this book.

'The Wedding' by Jean Sutherland of Newburgh, Fife 1970.
'Hallowe'en" by Violet Jacob from Bonnie Joann. Published by John Murray 1921.
'Harrowing Time' and 'Depression' from Gavin Greig's Folk-Song of The North East. Published by Folklore Associates, Harboro Pennsylvania 1963.